DOING GOOD
even
BETTER

DOING GOOD
even
BETTER

How to be an Effective Board Member of a Nonprofit Organization

EDGAR STOESZ

Former chair of Habitat for Humanity International

Intercourse, PA 17534
800/762-7171
www.GoodBooks.com

Dedicated to the memory of
WILLIAM T. SNYDER
Mennonite Central Committee
Executive Secretary
1957–1985
Servant leader
Mentor
Friend

Acknowledgments

Some writers acknowledge their publishers out of a sense of obligation. I acknowledge Good Books with a deep sense of deserved appreciation: Merle for insisting on presenting the book in an accessible manner; Phyllis for her excellent editing so that readers understand what I mean; Kate for helping the book find its audience; Cliff for designing the pages so clearly.

I also acknowledge the many who interacted with me on this important subject, either in response to one of my earlier books or in one of my workshops, or who served with me in some capacity. This books grows out of my interaction with many colleagues who like myself are striving to do good even better. From a long list I will name just two: Chester Raber with whom I co-authored *Doing Good Better* and long-time friend and Rick Stiffney who read the manuscript and offered helpful suggestions.

Pages 89–90, and Exhibits A., B., C., and D. (on pages 159–170), may be copied without requesting permission of the publisher. These are intended for active use by individual board members.

Drawing on page 114 by Cheryl Benner

Design by Cliff Snyder

DOING GOOD EVEN BETTER: HOW TO BE AN EFFECTIVE
BOARD MEMBER OF A NONPROFIT ORGANIZATION
Copyright ©2007 by Good Books, Intercourse, PA 17534
International Standard Book Number: 978-1-56148-601-4
Library of Congress Catalog Card Number: 2007031780

Library of Congress Cataloging-in-Publication Data

Stoesz, Edgar.
 Doing good even better : how to be an effective board member of a nonprofit organization / Edgar Stoesz.
  p. cm.
  ISBN-13: 978-1-56148-601-4 (alk. paper) 1. Nonprofit organizations--Management. 2. Directors of corporations. I. Title.
  HD62.6.S76 2007
  658.4'22--dc22   2007031780

Table of Contents

Preface

In 1994 I wrote *Doing Good Better* with my friend, Dr. Chester Raber. In 2000 I wrote *Common Sense for Board Members*. In **Doing Good Even Better: How to be an Effective Board Member of a Nonprofit Organization** I have brought the best of those earlier books together, and I've added what I have learned along the way since then.

Doing Good Even Better gives directors technical and tactical suggestions to increase their board-service effectiveness. I believe that one's *attitude* is as important as one's actions. Serving on a nonprofit board is:

- Duty—"To whom much has been given, much shall be required." It is a privilege to help others.
- Spontaneous—Act "as the spirit moves," and also with planning and practicing.
- An art form—Like playing jazz, as well as operating by the formulas that work.
- Idealistic, and down-to-earth practical.
- Giving and receiving in the spirit of St. Francis of Assisi who said, "It is in giving that we receive."
- Dead serious, and fun, most of the time.

One more thing. I am frequently asked, Do your suggestions and strategies for serving on a nonprofit board also apply to working in one's local church? Many nonprofit leaders are also congregational leaders, and most local churches face governance issues. *Doing Good Even Better* is directed to nonprofit organizations. On the other hand, much of what I say here also applies to congregations—with some adaptations.

Never think someone is
losing time by stopping to
sharpen his axe.

—*Abraham Lincoln*

PART I

Doing Good *Even* Better Begins with People

Nonprofit organizations are about people. People own them—for a purpose. People, with all their gifts and foibles, run them. Organizations do not run themselves. They are not run by something mysterious or extraterrestrial. Organizations are people work.

It follows logically that organizations are only as great as the people who are involved in them. They depend upon the synergy that results from the interaction of people who are reasonably of the same mind.

Remember that directors serve in a fiduciary capacity. They do not own; they hold in trust. The tangible and intangible assets of the organization are entrusted to the board for one purpose—to fulfill the purpose for which the organization exists.

Part I begins, therefore, by focusing on people—*who* should serve on a nonprofit board. I follow that by addressing *how* they should do their work, through program and procedures.

"Apart from people, an organization is only a shell. It knows nothing. It can do nothing. What an organization is capable of doing resides in the abilities of the people who run it."

−page 14

CHAPTER 1

Organizational Greatness Begins with People

In his highly acclaimed book *Good to Great,* Jim Collins suggests that the formula for organizational greatness is **a.**) getting the right persons on the bus, **b.**) getting the wrong persons off the bus, and **c.**) positioning them on the bus for maximum effectiveness. A clear, if not an easy, formula to achieve.

Would-be members of a great board must meet a three-fold test:

- *Personal qualifications*

  Is the potential director compatible with the organization's values and culture? Has s/he demonstrated genuine interest in its cause or similar causes? Is s/he self-aware and at peace with her-/himself and able to participate constructively in a group process while retaining independence of thought? Is her/his lifestyle in harmony with the organization?

  Beware of someone who brings her/his own agenda, who is interested in the task for all the wrong reasons. Beware of Lone Ranger directors. Board work is a team sport.

- ## *Proven competencies*

  What does the potential director know? What is s/he capable of doing? Do the demonstrated competencies of the board members encompass the entirety of the board's tasks?

  Apart from people, an organization is only a shell. It knows nothing. It can do nothing. What an organization is capable of doing resides in the abilities of the people who run it. Some skills can be hired in, but a board must have in its ranks persons who understand the big picture well enough to give direction to the total effort. Directorship is first and foremost about mature insight and proven judgment, and only secondarily about honors or prestige.

- ## *Representative*

  Does the prospective director represent the membership? A good nonprofit board has a mix of women and men, young and old, ethnicities, and the professions. Avoid being another old-boys club made up of gray-haired, white Protestant males. When your members review their board roster they should say, They represent me. I have confidence in them. This is especially important for nonprofits whose primary support comes from public appeals.

These three dimensions must be balanced according to the present circumstances when a board vacancy occurs. The need for a treasurer, for example, may be so urgent that other qualifications are put into secondary importance, but the ideal is always a board with a balanced representation of these three qualifications.

Assembling a great board begins with three things:

1. **Identifying persons who meet all three of the qualifications stated above.** Start by drawing up a wish list of persons, whether they're known to be available or not. Then trim to a short list based

on "fit." An alert Board Service Committee always has a list of prospects in reserve for such an occasion.

2. **Knowing well whom you are inviting.** Vet before you invite. Unless the individual is very well known by members of the Board Service Committee, it is necessary to have at least one personal interview. It is advisable to get references—perhaps including a police report or a credit rating. Boards should never find themselves in a position where they are so desperate to fill a board vacancy that they proposition someone before they are adequately acquainted with the individual. A board can readily terminate a CEO, but dislodging a seated director is difficult and can be messy.

> **When I ask the *right person*, at the *right time*, in the *right way*, I stand a good chance of getting the desired reply.**

3. **Asking.** Once the board has made its selection, how does it go about propositioning the candidate in such a way as to get an affirmative response? This is all an academic exercise until the candidate has confirmed acceptance. I find that when I ask the *right person*, at the *right time*, in the *right way*, I stand a good chance of getting the desired reply. In truth, I do not get many declinations, not because I am so persuasive, but because I am very selective in whom I ask, when, and how.

Timing the invitation

Do not ask someone who is about to have surgery or who has just had a major job change. Do not ask a CPA to become your treasurer during the tax season. Timing the invitation can make all the difference.

Consider carefully *how* you ask

Do not be overly casual. Give the invitation the air of importance it deserves. When I prepare to make a major request I do it in person, *always* in person. Not by telephone and never by e-mail. In some cases

I do it over a meal or at least a cup of coffee. Some deals, I am told, get consummated on the golf course. Do whatever works for you, but give careful consideration to how the invitation is made. Set the stage for the affirmative answer you want.

Finally, consider *who* should ask

I was present in a meeting recently where one member volunteered, "Permit me—he owes me big time!" He was deputized and got his trophy. Quid pro quo works. If you have a really big candidate in mind, have your Chair do the asking. That communicates the importance you want to convey.

One more suggestion. Don't dumb down the position, hoping to improve your chances of acceptance. That only sets the stage for a lukewarm director. Big people respond to big challenges. Small bait attracts little fish.

Follow-up your invitation with a letter summarizing the proposition and reiterating the invitation. Do it before the candidate has had an opportunity to reply. Keep the momentum moving in your favor.

Best wishes. Once you have great people on board, you are ready to do great things.

CHAPTER 2

Growing Great Directors

A successful nonprofit executive with whom I was privileged to work was fond of saying, "You take people for what they can do, and then supplement them (not criticize them) for what they are incapable of doing."

Effective organizations should make every effort to attract the best talent available to their boards. While some directors come ready-made, most are a work-in-progress. Nonprofits take directors as they are and then help them grow into all they can become.

I would rather have a board of inexperienced directors who are eager to work and learn, than a roster of "professional" directors who are interested primarily in the prestige of the office, and who sometimes come with baggage that is not helpful.

Jimmy and Rosalynn Carter's service to Habitat For Humanity International illustrates the value of a prestigious director. Bear in mind, however, that the Carters' value to Habitat resides in their authenticity. They come to build houses, not for a photo opportunity or to fatten their resumes.

Every board should have the personal growth of its directors as one of its conscious objectives. Departing directors should leave with new and better developed skills.

The benefits flow in both directions—directors become bigger, better people. It is their reward for having served. At the same time, highly qualified directors help the organization to become more effective.

Directors learn by doing

Call it in-service training. A director may be at mid-life, but a rookie where board directorship is concerned. Board service is an opportunity to develop new skills that may have application in other settings.

Directors learn by observing and interacting with others

But that happens only when directors make learning a conscious objective. Board service provides opportunities for directors to associate with and to observe successful people whom they might otherwise never meet, much less interact with. It permits them to see firsthand how others address issues and face problems. Board service is rich with networking opportunities. It can be tuition-free education. My life has been immeasurably enriched by what I have learned from fellow directors.

Directors learn by reading

Boards should periodically reward directors with a personal copy of a well-chosen book or magazine article. My reading list and thought life is continually being enriched by tips I pick up while associating with fellow directors.

Directors learn by moving around in a bigger world

Board service may at points take us outside our comfort zones, but that is where growth happens. Directors should visit project sites and interact with project leaders and participants. Boards should take field trips on occasion. For international organizations, this should include travel to foreign locations. Habitat for Humanity International conducts at least one board meeting in an overseas setting every two years. It helps directors make more informed decisions.

Every board should have the personal growth of its directors as one of its conscious objectives.

Bear in mind, however, that jetting a planeload of directors into the heart of Africa, or arranging for directors to spend an overnight in Harlem, unless accompanied by some advance reading and preparation, may be little more than water off a duck's back. As stated poignantly by John Erskine: "The body travels more easily than the mind, and until we have limbered up our imaginations, we continue to think as though we had stayed home. We have not really budged a step until we have taken up residence in someone else's point of view."

Directors learn from their mistakes

Mediocre boards try to hide their mistakes or explain them away. Effective boards own their mistakes and seek to learn from them. This requires that boards have an effective evaluation procedure in place by which mistakes (and successes) can be identified.

Directors learn through orientation

Good orientation is, without a doubt, a board's best training opportunity. Orientation can be an acceleration lane to effective board service. Never again will directors be so impressionable. Board tenure is limited, and unless efforts are made to move directors through the introductory stage quickly, they find themselves at mid-term before they are able to contribute significantly. Orientation is the ideal time to influence organizational culture—to purge the undesirable and replace it with what you seek to build.

New directors should be supplied with a packet of materials which includes a board roster, a copy of the bylaws, and recent annual reports.

During new-members' orientation they should be made aware of and encouraged to spend some time with the minute book and policy manual. There should be ample time for free-flowing questions and answers. Many boards include a well-selected book on board service in their orientation packet.

Freshman directors should be respectful of all that has gone before, but they should not be intimidated. From their first day on the job, their votes count for as much as the most senior director. Freshmen, in all their innocence, sometimes ask questions seniors are no longer asking. That may lead the board to do some things which senior directors had concluded were impossible. Freshmen have a unique role to play. They see with fresh eyes.

The benefits of director growth are reciprocal. Directors discover and develop new skills while the quality of board work increases, with the benefits radiating throughout the entire organization. Being part of a learning organization transforms what might otherwise be a mundane activity into one that is throbbing with excitement. That is board service at its best.

CHAPTER 3

Helping Directors Become Great Leaders

When boards do what comes naturally, they preserve and maintain. That has its place, but that is not a board's highest purpose. Boards exist to create, to explore, and to lead. Their concentration is equally on what does not yet exist, while keeping an eye on what is.

"Lead, follow, or get out of the way," says a bumper sticker. The world waits to be well led. In all endeavors—corporations, athletic teams, congregations or orchestras—leadership is key.

Leadership is filled with intangibles and ambiguities, and yet there are some universal principles that characterize great leadership.

1. **Leadership is about leading people.** Unlike technicians who master their trades, leaders specialize in giving direction to and motivating *people*. Great leaders are not those who are able to do the work of two or even 10, but are those who are able to lead an effort involving thousands. The capacity to lead people is among the most sought-after and rewarded human ability.

2. **The first responsibility of a leader, says Max DePree, is to define reality.** Leaders accept the present as their starting point.

Rudy Giuliani was elected mayor of New York when it was said to be an unmanageable city. He did not have the luxury of imagining New York as some idyllic middle-class suburb. He accepted New York as it was and proceeded to rehabilitate it with visible results.

3. **The best leaders are service-, not power-driven.** Leaders by definition have power, but they are most effective when they use it to empower others. Tom Peters in his book *Fast Company* states, "Great leaders don't create followers; they create more leaders."

> **A leader simply cannot be lethargic or pessimistic. That would be a contradiction.**

4. **Great leaders have high intellectual and physical energy that comes from passion, vision, and an optimistic spirit.** A leader simply cannot be lethargic or pessimistic. That would be a contradiction. Good leaders are able to see and believe in things before they exist.

5. **Leadership is, by definition, about affecting change.** To maintain, on the other hand, is to want to stay put. Making change successfully is a leader's greatest challenge.

6. **Great leaders are risk-takers.** Leadership involves navigating where there is no map, and sometimes not even a road. It involves putting trust in people before they have proven themselves. Robert Kennedy enjoyed quoting George Bernard Shaw who said, "...some men see things as they are and say why. I dream things that never were and say, Why not?"

7. **Leaders must be well matched to their tasks.** Even a strong leader fails when placed in a role that is not suited to him/her. A large, established nonprofit requires different leadership skills than an infant organization. Managing a used-clothing store requires different skills than managing a high-end jewelry store.

8. **Great leaders engender trust.** They are themselves worthy of trust. This requires them to be transparent and, to quote Jack Welsh in *Winning*, to "have not one iota of fakiness." People will not follow,

nor will they put out, for someone they do not trust. Where there is no trust, there can be no effective leadership. Trust is earned over time; it cannot be conferred or demanded.

For leadership to happen, there must be followers. Followers can make or break the leader. As there are leaders who don't lead, there are followers who don't follow, or who make leadership difficult, even impossible. Followership, like leadership, must be learned. Good followership is not synonymous with following blindly. Good leaders do not demand that. A successful leader once told me, "The best subordinate is not one who always agrees with me...surely not one who always disagrees with me...but one who gives me the confidence that together we will not err."

Is leadership learned, or are some born with it? In truth, leadership is both. Mature leaders do not suddenly appear out of nowhere. Some have more natural ability than others do, but in the end, leadership skill, like swimming, cannot be learned by reading about it. It is learned by doing. As seen in such giants as Winston Churchill, great leaders are formed as they perform their roles in the face of great challenges.

When selecting a leader, *beware* of someone who:
- Is quick to flaunt power and to take privilege for him/herself.
- Resorts to intimidation and manipulation.
- Is superficial.
- Is arrogant and personally ambitious.

President Woodrow Wilson once said, "Every man who assumes office in Washington either grows or swells." The same could be said of nonprofits. They are served best by servanthood leadership. Servant leaders are motivated not by power nor prestige, but by genuinely putting the interests of others and the cause ahead of themselves. By enabling rather than enforcing. Such is the leadership that people follow willingly and with good results.

No one said it better than the master teacher when instructing his disciples: "Whoever wants to be first must be last and servant of all."

CHAPTER 4

Making Room for Greatness

Some boards are so locked into inept, unmotivated directors—and into bad habits—that they become almost totally dysfunctional. I hesitate to address such a negative topic so early in what is basically a positive book. But it is sometimes necessary to eliminate negatives before it is possible to build on positives.

How does a board go about liberating itself from mediocrity, or worse? To say the obvious, boards cannot make the leap into greatness while sheltering lethargy, ineptitude, or destructive behaviors. I'll address later how wrong people get to be on a board, or how they move into this unfortunate category.

I know of no easy way to un-invite a sitting director. There is no one right way, but there are many wrong ways.

1. **Examine your motive.** Let it not be true—or be said—that your board disposes of those who do not give blanket approval to everything the leaders want.
2. **Count the cost.** The director in question may have sympathizers on the board or in the membership. In extreme cases, a lawsuit may develop. Be careful not to create a new problem or exacerbate an existing one. Live by the physician's code—"Do no harm."

Sometimes it may not be worth deposing a poorly functioning member.

3. Issues related to board membership and performance are the board's responsibility and must be addressed by the board (usually in the person of the Chair or Board Service Committee), not the CEO. The CEO is responsible *to* the board, not *for* the board.

4. Be compassionate. "Do unto others as..." See it from the perspective of the board member in question: "I gave all those years and this is what I get!"

5. Address the situation firmly and yet directly, not circuitously. Do not engineer a board resolution that describes the person in question without naming her/him. Do not serve notice by email. Unpleasant as it is, matters like this must be dealt with under four or six eyes, to borrow a German metaphor.

6. Provide an honorable alternative. Allow the director in question to withdraw his/her name or to resign. You may want to offer some severance inducement, but in doing so be careful not to dig yourself into another hole.

7. Consider timing. Don't tackle so contentious an issue days before a holiday, or when the person in question is dealing with other trauma, or when your board agenda is overloaded with other controversial issues.

Taking all of these qualifiers into consideration, if you still feel that action is needed, do it! The job will probably never get easier, and it might get harder and costlier.

I dreaded processing the retirement of a senior field worker who had been valuable, but also difficult at times. I worked hard to have his wife present in the meeting since the two of them had served together. I went to considerable effort to have his whole retirement package assembled. I scheduled the interview when I thought they might be most receptive—not at the end of a tired day. It went well. They felt cared for, not discarded.

Most directors, by the time they have served six or eight years, have contributed most of what they have to offer and should graciously step aside to make room for their successors.

Once you have worked your way through this difficult problem, consider how you can prevent it from recurring. Problems related to involuntary retirement have a lot to do with expectations. Most directors begin their board service in a mood of humility, even timidity. Somewhere along the line, some come to assume that, This position belongs me. When that assumption is called into question, the mood changes fast, usually resulting in bad feelings and disruption. Here are a few suggestions that may help to prevent these problems from occurring:

1. **Do better at managing board members' expectations.** Emphasize that board membership is *service*. The cause is bigger than any one person. Do not allow re-upping to be assumed or seen as automatic. Additional terms must be earned by performance. Directors should never be allowed to rest on past laurels.

2. **Consider term or age limits.** Such limits are, in my estimation, among the best of less-than-perfect options. They are admittedly arbitrary and may on occasion result in the retirement of a director who is still productive. On the positive side, term limits serve notice that directors have a limited timeframe within which to make their contributions. Most directors, by the time they have served six or eight years, have contributed most of what they have to offer and should graciously step aside to make room for their successors. Directors who stay too long too often end up subtracting from the good work they have done and make the transition to new members difficult.

3. **Institute a board-service pledge.** In it, directors are required to state their intent to make a good transition to their successors when

the time comes to step down. Seeing such a pledge practiced by fellow directors helps sitting directors to prepare psychologically for retirement.

You should now have the right people seated around your board table. They are the ones who will create the agenda by which the organization will deliver on its contract with its members.

The next challenge is to create an environment that is conducive to individual board members' personal growth and synergistic interaction to advance the cause.

DISCUSSION QUESTIONS
FOR A BOARD'S LEADERS

1. Do a quick assessment of your board. Are there any obvious gaps in representation or in skills that should be filled by new appointments?

2. Review your organization's plans for the succession of directors and officers. Is continuity provided for, or will a transition find the board ill-prepared?

3. Are there persons on your board who are not carrying their weight? Are any a hindrance or a distraction? If so, what plans does your board have for their rehabilitation or replacement?

4. Does your board have a Board Service Committee that has two primary tasks: identifying and nominating candidates for election to the board after carefully screening them, and leading the board in an annual self-evaluation process? If not, should the board consider naming such a committee? For some boards, this may be the expansion of an existing nominating committee.

    When I chaired the Habitat for Humanity International board, I was an ex officio member of all committees except the Board Service Committee. The Chair was excluded from that committee because the performance of the Chair, as well as the performance of all directors, and their continuation in office, was subject to the evaluation of this committee. It is one of the most influential committees on any board.

5. Review your plans for board training. How will you in this year help directors individually, and collectively as a board, grow into greater effectiveness?

6. Review your new-member orientation program. Does it adequately convey your board's plans and priorities for the future? Does it draw newly elected directors into effective board service?

PART II

Helping Directors Understand Their Governance Role

Many directors get off on the wrong foot because they do not understand the difference between governance and management. Many boards are described with embarrassing accuracy by the German proverb: "Everyone is doing as they want; no one is doing what they should; but everyone is enthusiastically involved." Good people, all with the best of intentions, but confused about their roles.

In this section I will first make the governance/management distinction. Perhaps it helps to think of this in governmental terms. Governance could be compared with the Congressional branch; management with the Executive branch. Both are needed. We are describing a partnership where each is fulfilled and completed by the other. To be effective, both need to understand this distinction between their two roles and live by it.

Having made this important distinction, I identify six practical functions a board performs in the exercise of its governance role.

Don't miss Exhibit A., Board Self-Evaluation: Board Responsibilities—The Full Scope, when you've finished reading this section.

"Many organizations, sad to say, live too much in the present. I believe that the board's domain is the future."

—*page 40*

CHAPTER 5

Distinguishing Governance from Management

A board's role is to *govern*. To exercise the authority conferred on it by the members. It is to make decisions and set in motion a process by which member expectations are met. It is to discern, to think, to exercise judgment, to plan. Board work is headwork; hands are optional.

This is distinct from management, whose role is to *implement* decisions and plans approved by the board. Whereas the board decides *ends* (outcomes), management is responsible for the *means* by which ends are achieved. In governmental terms, the board is the Legislative branch (Congress) while management is the Executive branch (the President).

In practice, the board and management work in concert with each other. Each is completed by the other. The German proverb says it well: "One hand washes the other." The diagram below illustrates this important distinction.

The BIG X

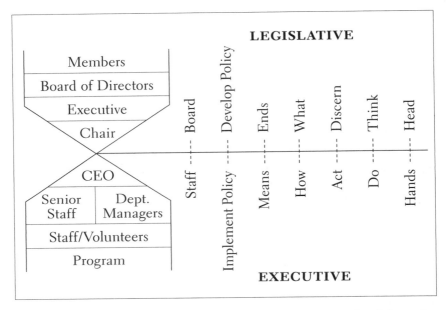

The line separating the board and management should not be thought of as an immovable stone wall. Directors need to know what is happening below the line. And management should be permitted input into board governance decisions above the line. This is a partnership in which each understands and respects its role and the role of the other. Each is completed by the other. But the two roles are distinct, and that distinction must be understood and respected throughout the organization.

Directors may—indeed directors *should*—visit project sites. They may even participate in a work activity. But they must always remember that when directors serve *as volunteers*, they do so *without* board authority. Inversely, when staff address the board, they do so respecting the board's right to decide. Management must not intrude into the board's governance role. Directors must not micromanage.

When as chair of Habitat For Humanity International, I participated in the annual Jimmy Carter blitz-build, I took orders from the house foreman. I was a volunteer, and my board role was beside the point. The blitz-build was not a board event. I was, pure and simple, a volunteer like several hundred others.

Whereas the board decides *ends* (outcomes), management is responsible for the *means* by which ends are achieved.

To illustrate: The decision of a school district to open a pre-school or a middle school would be made by the school district's board. The board would also give further policy instructions as it deems necessary. Beyond that, management is responsible to implement the board decision within those policies established by the board.

The board of Mennonite Central Committee, an international relief agency where I once served on the staff, may decide to open a program in Zimbabwe. It may state that the program shall focus on HIV/Aids, or whatever, with specific goals and objectives. It may also state the project's annual budget, the number of workers, and so on. Beyond that, management is authorized to implement the action within approved policies, reporting back as agreed.

Young or small organizations seldom make this governance/management distinction. Everybody works until the work is done, or until they fall over from exhaustion. As organizations grow and mature, boards need to have less hands-on involvement and concentrate more on governing through the programs, values, and policies they adopt, the implementation of which is under the direction of management.

Failure to make this distinction consistently results in overburdening the board, while management is demoralized and uncertain about its role. Boards which are involved in operations at the expense of their governance function are an impediment and perpetually on the verge of exhaustion.

Before a board can be effective, it must understand its governance role as distinct from management. That understanding may change over time, but directors should be constantly mindful of the difference in functions.

When this governance/management distinction is understood and practiced, board work is more effective. Meetings are shorter, more productive, and enjoyable. When boards are clear about their role, the rest falls in line. When a board is unclear about its role, confusion and misunderstanding abound. Role clarity begins with the board.

The next six essays discuss in more detail and in practical terms what board governance means.

CHAPTER 6

Defining the Purpose—Duty #1

To be effective, an organization should begin by stating—in clear and compelling terms—the purpose for which it exists. That statement will identify what the board in its fiduciary capacity is undertaking to accomplish on behalf of the members. This purpose statement should address three questions. The board of directors should be ever mindful of those same three questions:

1. **What do our members expect?** Why do members support the effort? Good directors listen. They have their ears to the ground. They invite interaction.

    Members have expectations, although they are seldom in written form. Directors must tease those expectations out of them by taking careful note of what members do or do not support, what they value, what they will not tolerate, and whom they elect. Member expectations will likely change over time. And there will likely be occasions on which directors must educate members. But in the end, an organization is viable only if its activities are understood and supported by its members.

2. **What need are we addressing?** This line of inquiry will help to answer Peter Drucker's rhetorical question, "What is our business?"

A board answers this question by stating the vision and mission that will guide program formation.

Nonprofit organizations always exist in response to a defined need. Needs abound, and so do organizations to address them! In the United States and Canada there are more than a million nonprofit organizations, each focused on a defined need. The needs can be as varied as Mothers Against Drunk Driving and The Preservation of Covered Bridges. Directors must identify the particular need expressed by their members.

3. **What are our resources?** What do we have, or what can we get by way of staff, money, and/or material, by which to address this need meaningfully? What do we know, and what are we competent to do? Organizations must resist the temptation to be all things to all people, to chase popular causes, to overestimate themselves and underestimate what is needed. Nothing is served by do-gooders undertaking activities that are outside of their competency or resources.

Having answered these foundational questions, a board should address in greater depth the issues of vision, mission, and values.

Vision states the purpose for which an organization exists and for what it wants to *become*. Vision imagines something that is not yet but could be. Vision drives out the status quo. It liberates organizations from old routines and gives them a reason to exist. To borrow from Robert Browning, "Our reach must exceed our grasp or what's a heaven for?"

Average boards orient themselves around what they see in their rearview mirrors. Precedent is their guiding principle.

In defining its vision, an organization sets aside everyday limitations and frustrations to imagine what it wants most to become. The best vision statements are bold and concise. Once a vision statement is adopted, it becomes the standard against which actions are measured.

While I chaired the American Leprosy Missions board, we adopted a vision statement that consists of just seven words: "Christ's servants, freeing the world of leprosy." It identified us as Christ's servants who seek not to minister to persons with leprosy, but to free the world of this dreaded disease. Seven bold words gave focus and energy to our effort.

Average boards orient themselves around what they see in their rearview mirrors. Precedent is their guiding principle. Average boards examine everything under the microscope. They want to avoid mistakes. Great boards look through a telescope to planets beyond. They look at what could be and ask, Why not?

Mission is what an organization commits itself to *do*. It identifies a clear, compelling, and achievable goal. Whereas a vision is a dream, a stretch, mission is a commitment: "This we will do." For many years, Habitat used the tagline, "Building houses with God's people in need." Whereas vision reaches for the stars, mission is grounded in the here and now. Organizations need both: Vision to identify the more distant goal; mission to identify the means by which the identified vision is realized.

I notice that vision and mission statements have a tendency to run together, to not be clearly different. A vision statement should identify the strategic goal, while the organization's mission is embodied in the annual work plan, admittedly much longer than a statement.

Values. Great organizations are not only concerned about getting things done, they want things done in ways that are consistent with their stated values. Habitat For Humanity is more than another construction company. It is concerned that the houses it builds are owned and occupied by deserving families who will care for them. It is concerned about the communities within which these families reside. It seeks to put the issue of affordable housing on the minds and consciences of everyone, and to look for ways to influence public policy on behalf of the poor. It wants to be known as a Christian ministry.

Management participates with the board both in defining the purpose for which an organization exists and in designing programs by which the purpose will be achieved in accordance with stated values.

A clear and compelling sense of purpose gives an organization energy that propels it to do great things. If a journey begins with a destination, an organization begins by knowing for what purpose it exists.

CHAPTER 7

Planning to Fulfill the Purpose—Duty #2

After a board has clarified the purpose for which it exists, it must devise a plan to achieve that purpose. Vision and mission statements are only fine-sounding phrases until they are put into operation.

Planning is the link between what is and what is to be. It is the gateway to the future.

Planning should be part of every board's annual routine. Great boards periodically set aside routine business that presents itself with undeserved urgency, in order to concentrate on formulating a plan by which its identified purpose will be realized. This requires determination and discipline. It is a necessary step in the pathway to greatness. Organizations exist to *do*, and for that they need to plan.

Organizations that fail to plan, plan to fail.

Organizations need both a long-range plan *and* an *annual* work plan. The two are related but distinct.

The long-range plan reaches beyond what is possible today and aspires to vistas unrealized. The process of planning identifies a need before the capacity is there to address it. It entertains what is not yet possible and visualizes what is to be. Plans should be bold, but within the realm of what is or will become possible.

Visionary planning drives out the status quo. It liberates organizations from drowsy routines and gives them a reason to exist. Vision is focused on the future.

Because the focus of long-range planning is distant, it must be somewhat general in nature. This is in contrast to annual planning which must be specific. A hospital board may imagine the addition of satellite clinics, but the location of those clinics and the level of care they will provide will be addressed later in the annual work plan. The board of a thrift store should anticipate the need for an expanded building to accommodate increased volume years before its location is known. Planning can be thought of as walking with an idea or living in the dream until it becomes a reality.

Many organizations, sad to say, live too much in the present. I believe that the board's domain is the future. If by some stroke of good fortune, most nonprofits were to unexpectedly receive a million dollars, they wouldn't know what to do with it. They think and plan in small increments. They have no plans beyond the immediate, or their planning horizon is too short. Instead of a boost, a sudden infusion of funds would be a problem that might cause them to do something foolish. Remember, your reach should exceed your grasp.

The annual work plan is a commitment—"This we will do. Count on it." It is not enough to be busy. Everyone is already as busy as they can be. Organizations need to be specific about what they want to *accomplish*. Drawing from the identified long-range plan, the annual work plan establishes specific goals and activities by which the vision will be realized. It states what will be done (outcomes), who will do it, where, with how much, by when, and with what. Its progress can be monitored and measured.

The annual planning process begins by evaluating how the program is performing. It asks, What should we be doing more of? Less of? What is working well? What is leaving us disappointed? What is wearing out? It selects those activities that will contribute toward fulfilling the organization's long-range plan. It takes note of what will be needed by way of staff, money, and facilities and ensures their availability.

The long-range and the annual work plans function in concert with each other. The long-range plan creates the context from which the annual plan is drawn and toward which it aspires.

Planning is dynamic

Planning is not once said and then done. President Eisenhower frequently said, "The plan is nothing; planning is everything." This suggests that planning is ongoing, subject to change when circumstances change. A five-year plan, for example, is not expected to last five years. It should be reviewed annually and changed as suggested by experience. Stated another way, organizations should always be in the first year of a multi-year plan.

Tom Peters warns in a similar vein against holding plans too tightly. Plans are servant, not master. Plans belong to us, not we to them. They should be changed as the circumstances to which they apply change, but activity should always be guided by a plan, within the context of a long-term plan.

The exercise of planning is another opportunity for board/management collaboration. Both have a role in planning. Whereas the board sets the context and identifies the more distant goals (above the line), management is responsible for plan implementation. In mature organizations with professional staff, management may recommend the annual plan to the board, based on the board-approved long-range plan and other instructions provided by the board. Once approved, the plan is delegated to management for implementation.

Organizations that fail to plan, plan to fail.

CHAPTER 8

Delegating Responsibility for Plan Implementation—Duty #3

After clarifying its purpose, after devising plans by which the mission and vision will be realized, the board should next delegate responsibility for implementing the plan. It is through implementation of the plan that a board discharges its fiduciary responsibility to its members.

Boards do not generally implement plans they make. Implementation happens by delegating. Delegating is a separate and distinct activity that is often neglected or taken for granted. If planning answers the *what*, delegation addresses the *how* and *who*. Good plans can be wasted by careless implementation.

Good plans can be wasted by careless implementation.

Delegation is a multi-step process.

1.   **Delegation begins with clarifying *what* shall be done.** This is the link between planning and action.

---

2. **Delegation identifies intended outcomes.** What is to be accomplished? Outcomes are what members expect of their nonprofit organizations.

3. **Delegation states by when something is to be done.** This may involve setting up a multi-year schedule that can be monitored.

4. **Delegation establishes who is responsible for an activity.** Plan implementation is generally assumed to be a management, below-the-line responsibility, under the direction of the CEO. In young or small organizations, delegation may be given to a board committee(s). Directors may elect to do as much as they have energy for, or as may be necessary under the circumstances. In so doing, however, they must be careful not to neglect or become confused about their governance function, or to conflict with staff.

5. **Delegation requires accompanying instructions, more commonly known as policies.** Too often the unspoken assumption is, Do as you think best. Some even infer, Don't bother us with the details.

    Board policies delineate the realm within which management is authorized to function. Visually, I think of policies as buoys. The challenge is to make them specific enough to give practical guidance, yet not so detailed as to restrict the rightful role and discretion of management. This is illustrated in the drawing on page 114.

    Each board must decide for itself what "buoys" are needed and useful, and what guidance it wants to give management as part of the implementation process.

6. **Delegation involves supervision.** The effective delegator does not give authorization and then disappear, assuming all will be well. Effective delegators back away and allow the process to work, but they stay in touch. This can easily tip into micromanagement, which directors must avoid. At the same time, directors must not back away so completely that they become disconnected from what is happening. This is another organizational ambiguity that great boards learn to navigate.

The Mennonite Central Committee (MCC) disaster-response policy, which I was responsible to administer, stated simply that MCC's first response is through people, then money. Staff were instructed not to send money until an on-the-scene assessment had been made. Then personnel were sent with money and material as needed. We were usually not the first to arrive on the scene of a disaster, but we were often among the last to leave. Policy establishes the niche within which management is authorized to act.

Effective delegators back away and allow the process to work, but they stay in touch.

Sometimes a program failure can be traced to inadequate board oversight. It was reported to an international board which I chaired that one of our national programs had experienced a misappropriation of funds. Our impulse was to be irritated with staff for sloppy management that allowed this to happen. We were further nonplussed to discover that the operations had never been audited. How sloppy can you get! we thought. Only then were we informed that the board had never mandated that field programs were to be audited. We made amends by adopting a board policy directing that all major field programs be audited annually.

Boards should specify what they expect in major areas before a lapse occurs.

Policies restrict but they also liberate

Some boards excuse themselves for not adopting policies by contending that policies restrict staff. Policies are admittedly a restriction of sorts, but I prefer to view them as guidelines. Policies help staff to know what is expected. They define the realm within which staff is free to function with board approval. Policies increase overall efficiency because they prevent reinventing the wheel. There must always be provision for exceptions to policy when circumstances warrant, and policies need to be revised periodically, but all major activity should be regulated by policy.

Board policies should be assembled in a policy manual and available for quick reference. Policies are helpful only if they are available in a timely fashion.

Having delegated responsibility for the implementation of their plans, with accompanying instructions (policies) as necessary, directors who know their role step back and let things work. They do not interfere or micromanage. They do not meddle or second-guess. They observe and, after an appropriate interval, they evaluate. Effective delegation checks back—How is it going? What have we learned? What might we do differently? The results of the evaluation are then cycled back into the planning format. That is how good organizations end up doing good *even* better.

CHAPTER 9

Resourcing the Plan—Duty #4

Directors have a fiduciary responsibility to safeguard an organization's assets and to use them efficiently in the fulfillment of its stated purpose. This includes both ledger and non-ledger assets.

One of the best treasurers I was privileged to know often said, "Money isn't everything, but it sure beats whatever is in second place." Spoken typically as a treasurer, but not without a point. Money is important—anyone questioning that should try running an organization without it. But an organization's resources go beyond money and include both ledger and non-ledger assets.

Ledger Assets

These assets refer to the management of money and physical facilities. Day-to-day money-management functions are delegated to management, but directors are expected to exercise prudent oversight of all ledger assets. Boards commonly do this through the following practices:

- Approval of an annual budget that distributes funds in accordance with plans approved by the board, with appropriate financial reporting throughout the year.

- An annual independent financial audit with follow-up as necessary.
- Prudent risk and cash-flow management procedures. For example: all income is to be deposited. All disbursements are to be by check. Bank accounts are to be balanced by someone other than persons assigned to issue checks. And so on.

Boards are responsible to insure that the resources are available to carry out the plans they have approved. Budgets must be brought into balance either by increasing income or decreasing expenditures. The identification of such imbalances is precisely one of the functions of budgeting. Related functions, such as fund-raising and accounting, may be delegated to staff or committees of the board, but responsibility resides with the board.

"Money isn't everything, but it sure beats whatever is in second place."

To approve a plan or budget without the requisite resources in hand, or without a realistic plan to raise them, is irresponsible. Board members are also expected to support fund-raising efforts and to contribute personally in proportion to their means.

Non-Ledger Assets

These assets are less visible, but they may be even more important than hard assets. I think of them under two categories:

1. **Personnel.** You are only as good as your help, says my Amish neighbor. How true it is! The ability to attract and retain strong staff separates the good from the great. Much of this responsibility resides below the line with management, but there is a role for the board as well. Board responsibility in this vital organizational area is discharged through mandating the following procedures:

- Job descriptions for all positions, written with outcomes in mind, and not merely activities. (Who is responsible to do what?)
- An organizational chart to describe relationships. (Who is responsible to whom?)
- An annual performance-appraisal procedure, beginning with the CEO, but in place throughout the whole organization. (How well are we doing?)
- A salary and benefit scale, including a personal-growth plan for all employees. (How much pay/benefits?)
- A grievance procedure to be followed when things go wrong, as they will even in the best organizations.
- Exit interviews. Much can be learned by knowing why people leave their employment. The board or a committee of the board may not read each exit interview report, but the board should require that such a procedure is in place, and it should reserve the right to read such reports when circumstances appear to warrant doing so.

2. **Image and Reputation.** Solomon did not talk about brands, but he underscored the importance of reputation when he said, "A good name is better than great riches." This is especially apropos for nonprofits that depend on public support. Reputation is earned over many years, and it can be lost in one careless act.

It is no longer good enough for nonprofits to go quietly about doing a good job. Healthy charities look for appropriate ways to promote and safeguard their brands. Image must be built, protected, promoted. It is one of the most valuable assets a public charity has.

Survival and delivery of services are an organization's ultimate test. To serve, organizations must survive. To survive, organizations must serve. Survival does not mean just getting by. To be healthy, organizations need to thrive. The public wants and deserves bang for the buck. Obsolescence, sloth, and apathy must be avoided like the plague.

Adopting a grandiose plan without providing the enabling resources serves no purpose. It is sheer folly. A plan is good only if it is accompanied with the resources needed for its fulfillment. This is another area where board and management must collaborate, but ultimately the board is responsible to ensure that resources are there to complete the plan it approves and promotes.

CHAPTER 10

Monitoring and Evaluating— Duty #5

It is not enough for boards to approve and delegate. Directors must continually be asking, Is it happening? Are we delivering on our "contract" with our members? When assessing what is going on, directors should be neither too superficial nor self-congratulatory.

Monitoring

Directors have numerous sources of information by which they can determine if the program they have adopted is being implemented and if it is producing the desired results.

- Personal observation. I've heard it referred to by the acronym NIFO—Nose In, Fingers Out. Board members should make it their duty to observe what is happening; however, without getting in the way. They should visit the office or project sites at appropriate times. They should attend open-house ceremonies and other public events without fail. They should inquire of others in the know and keep their ears to the ground without appearing to be snooping.

- Staff reports. Boards should insist on the reports that they need in order to discharge their oversight responsibilities. Reports must be comprehensible. They must permit the tracking of progress. Without the ability to compare, statistics are meaningless. Most boards don't need more information; they need right information.

  Directors should read staff reports appreciatively, but also with a measure of skepticism, mindful of the tendency to under-report failure and over-report success. They should be wary when suddenly all is quiet. Perceptive directors read both what is on the line and what is between the lines.

- Outside audits. External audits are routine in the financial area. I fail to understand why nonprofits don't use them more in the vital program area. A review may be either by a professional consultant or by a respected peer, perhaps on a reciprocal basis. For example, I know parochial schools, as well as Habitat affiliates and MCC Thrift Shops, learn much from each other—when the opportunity is provided.

Key metrics may be monitored by using the following tracking devices:

> **Most boards don't need more information; they need right information.**

1. A "dashboard" that identifies on one page the key facts you want to track. This technique helps to see at a glance what activities may be soaring or slumping, and then to take corrective action if needed.

2. **A timeline that sequences a multi-phased activity and states the date by which each is to be completed.** It, too, helps to see at a glance when an activity is falling behind schedule.

Evaluating

Are the organization's activities producing the desired outcomes? It cannot be assumed that value in is value out. Some efforts are an out and out waste of time and money, or a lost opportunity. Boards need to evaluate three spheres of activity:

1. **Board members themselves.** Begin with the evaluation most board members are least willing to undertake.
    - Remembering that meetings are where a board does its work, begin by asking, How productive are our meetings?
    - Is the board making decisions, or is it primarily approving reports? Are the board's decisions good ones?
    - Is the board proactively engaging the future, or is it living on past laurels?
    - Are all directors pulling their weight, or is there dead wood?
    - Is provision being made for leadership continuity/transition and for director development?

    Remember, organizations, like trees, die from the top.

2. **The CEO.** S/he is the only person directly responsible to the board. All other staff report to the CEO. They are evaluated by, or under the direction of, the CEO. The board's review of its CEO should include the following:
    - Affirmation. Identify and acknowledge good performance.
    - Identify areas where performance is lacking, and together agree on a plan for improvement.
    - Review salary, benefits, training, and tenure intentions.

    CEO performance reviews should be summarized in writing and reported to the board in executive session.

3. **The program.** Remember, organizations exist to do. Insecure management feels threatened when a board requests program evaluation, and they may resist it. Management may accuse the board of lacking trust or of engaging in micromanagement. Such an attitude is not a good sign. Strong management welcomes the board's involvement in program evaluation.

    In fairness, boards sometimes approach program evaluation awkwardly. Some do it with a "Got ya!" mentality. Their attitude may be, Make management shape up, thinking (mistakenly) that by such power tactics they are correcting things. In this frame of mind they are likely doing more harm than good.

Directors have a right, a need, to know:

- Is the mission happening? (Outcomes)
- How could it happen better? (Self-improvement)
- What is winding down/wearing out? (Vulnerabilities)
- What is waiting for its turn? (Vision—opportunities)
- Are we well positioned for the future? (Dreaming)

Program evaluation is complete only after these findings have been cycled back into the annual planning process.

Evaluation affords an opportunity to extend and to deepen the board/management partnership, since both need to participate in the exercise. While management is closer to program realities, an informed board has a more objective point of view. In the evaluation process, trust and relationships between board and management can be strengthened. Evaluation is an essential part of making the leap from passable to outstanding.

Remember, organizations, like trees, die from the top.

(For a fuller discussion of evaluations see Part IV.)

CHAPTER 11

Reporting Back to the Members—Duty #6

Directors do not own the enterprise; the members do. Directors are trustees acting on behalf of the members, and that includes donors. It follows logically that directors are responsible to report back to the "owners."

Many nonprofit boards would benefit by making a greater effort to better understand their membership. Community-based organizations, like schools or hospitals, are literally surrounded by their members, and therefore know what they expect. Feeling accountable to a national or international membership is more difficult but no less necessary. Some boards commission a membership profile in order to have a better grasp of who they are. Knowing its members, and staying in a meaningful discussion with them, must remain a constant board preoccupation.

Healthy nonprofits maintain good communication with their members. Members receive a steady flow of reports that feature both accomplishments and disappointments. Too many nonprofits communicate with their members only when they are asking for more money. Nonprofits show their insecurity when they underestimate the ability of their members to accept and understand a program reversal. Trusting the membership with the news that something went wrong can, if well done, deepen trust and support. When problems are glossed over or ignored, or worse, denied, the membership can become cynical and suspicious.

Community-based organizations have an advantage because they are able to report to and thank members for their support in person. Reporting to members that are scattered and at a great distance must be done through indirect means, including the Internet. Regardless of what medium is used, reports must be factual. They should be rich in human-interest material, including especially how lives were changed by an activity. An abbreviated version of the audited financial statement should be included since finances are on members' minds.

This is an area in which nonprofits can learn from for-profit companies, who address their annual report to their stockholders. The nonprofit equivalent is to address the annual report to the members, demonstrating the accountability that directors have to them. Instead, nonprofits are likely to attach their annual report to a fund-raising hard sell. That approach eventually wears out and leaves contributors feeling unthanked.

Respectfully addressing members as "owners" carries a strong psychological message. It is an acknowledgment of accountability that builds and deepens member loyalty.

Too many nonprofits communicate with their members only when they are asking for more money.

Good reporting creates respect and trust, which has huge benefits for fund-raising, even in the absence of a direct request. Fund-raisers know that present contributors are their best prospects for future gifts. How much they give to any one of the many deserving causes that appeal to them depends on how well the contributors have been drawn into the organizations' particular spheres. Effective reporting lays a foundation, it builds confidence and trust, and it earns an organization the right to ask for continued, even increased, support.

Nonprofit boards should give deliberate thought to how they report to their members. Good reports build trust, and trust builds support. Money and effort invested in keeping members well informed can be viewed as both a duty and an investment in the future. Maintaining a strong relationship with its membership is essential for a nonprofit's health and vitality.

Evaluating Your Board's Performance

How could you improve your board's execution of these six primary board duties? Take the time to complete Exhibit B., Board Self-Evaluation: Board Duties—How Well Are We Accomplishing Them? The exercise will direct your attention to areas where your board needs to improve.

Changing habits of long standing is never easy, but it's a necessary part of doing good *even* better. You know the old mantra—"If you do what you've always done, you will get what you always got." The best *time* to start is now. The best *place* to start is with yourself. Make a list of things you resolve to do better or differently, and then do them. Once begun, the next challenge is to make this new behavior a habit, meeting after meeting performing better and better.

Your next step is to address change that needs to be made by the *full* board, since board service is a *team* sport. Many boards develop bad habits that leave them, if not entirely dysfunctional, functioning only at a fraction of their capacity. As a result, they fail to attract good people, and without good people they are caught in a downward spiral. This can be arrested by creating an occasion (perhaps a retreat) when the entire board looks at itself and reviews how it is functioning.

Regardless of how well you and the full board are functioning, there is always room for improvement. It is through self-evaluation that good boards become better. Improvement at the board level is ultimately reflected throughout the whole organization. Soon the entire organization will function better. Organizational improvement begins with the board.

Remember, while many things are outside of a board's control, the way in which a board does business—including, how it spends its time—is entirely its own doing. Boards deserve what they get.

PART III

Helping Boards Have Better Meetings

A board functions as a board only when it is in session, only when it is having a meeting. It is generally true that the quality of a board's meetings is reflected in the quality of its work. Great boards have great meetings. It is as simple as that!

Unless meetings are well planned and conducted, they can be a colossal waste of time. Twelve directors meeting for three hours constitutes nearly one work week. The results do not always justify the investment of time and effort. My hunch is that nonprofits would use board and committee meeting time better if they had to pay for it.

Not only are many meetings a waste of time, some meetings are destructive. Instead of serving as a springboard for the action to follow, they leave members frustrated and dispirited, never wanting to see the inside of a boardroom again. I know, too, that many CEOs' use of Alka Seltzer increases when board-meeting time comes around. This should not be, nor is it necessary.

Board meetings can be enjoyable, inspiring, and invigorating. They are that only if good procedures are followed, and if there is a united spirit within the board membership.

Boards are held accountable even for things that are outside their control. Unfair but true. One thing that is entirely within a board's control is how it does business. Boards deserve the meetings they have.

CHAPTER 12

Meetings—Why Have Them?

"**M**adame Chair, I move that until further notice, we discontinue all board meetings." The imaginary motion would probably fail for lack of a second. But how necessary are board meetings? Why have them? What are they expected to accomplish? After all, they take up a lot of time, and, unless they are well planned and conducted, they are a waste of valuable time.

Remember that a board functions as a board **only** when it is convened and having a meeting. The boardroom is the board's workshop. That is where it does its work. But for what purpose? What are board meetings expected to accomplish? Why are they necessary?

Meetings have only two purposes: to inform and to make decisions. Everything else—call it socializing or whatever takes up your meeting time—is not board business.

To inform and to be informed

Good decisions are based on skillfully gathering and analyzing information, not going with lucky hunches. Good fact-gathering and analysis reduce the risk inherent in all decision-making.

Most information comes to the board from staff, usually in a meeting or in preparation for a meeting. The information must meet the following tests:

- Is it reliable? Information on a given subject must be comprehensive and inclusive of both positives and negatives. Decisions can only be as good as the information on which they are predicated.

- Is it comprehensible? Directors should insist that reports, including financial reports, be understandable. The monthly treasurer's report to a board I chaired was computer-generated and ran to six pages. It was hard to follow, and it left me and the whole committee feeling illiterate. Such reports are not only useless, they are dangerous. They give the appearance of reporting, while still leaving everyone in the dark. Our board was better served by a one-page report that concentrated on the essentials.

- Is it well organized? Facts and figures that are well assembled suggest their own conclusions. At least they point us in the right direction. With rare exceptions, a report should be limited to one page with attachments as needed.

- Does the report state what action is expected? Reports should state early on if it is for information only, or if action is anticipated. If action is expected, the desired action should be stated in a recommendation. Honoring this simple procedure can save hours of meeting time and frustration and lead to better decisions.

A board functions as a board only when it is convened and having a meeting.

My goal in reporting is to anticipate and answer questions before they are asked. When the board processes a well-prepared report, the resulting action may appear to an outsider to be so perfunctory as to be merely rubber-stamping. Not necessarily. It may be that the board got the information it needed, thus eliminating the need for much discussion.

Decision-Making

This is the second purpose of a meeting. Some boards do little more than receive and approve reports, with deep appreciation, of course. They make few decisions of any consequence. Either nothing is happening, or the decision-making process is circumventing the board. Both are troublesome signs.

Nor is it good when boards are maneuvered into a position where they appear to have no choice but to approve what is being recommended. They may be faced with a tight deadline, or other options have been precluded. Either the board and/or management is doing a poor job of anticipating when an action is needed, or the board is being set up. Such a situation should not happen often.

Boards do not make good decisions when in one session they are expected to take a raw issue and work it up to the point of making a decision. This requires an inordinate amount of meeting time, or it results in a cobbled-together compromise that does not meet the next-day test.

Issues that are too complex to be dealt with on the spot, or that are presented in unfinished form, should be assigned to a committee or to management for study and re-submission before being allowed to wreck the agenda. Material must always be well analyzed and presented to the board in a proposal form, ready to be acted upon.

This procedure requires boards to be skillful in processing proposals presented to them by a committee or management. (See Exhibit F. Writing Effective Proposals for Board Action.) The tendency is to follow one of two extremes. Either directors feel obligated to approve a proposal, even though serious questions remain, or they sweep the preliminary work aside and re-do the work of the committee. The former is superficial; the latter wasteful. The ability to take a complex issue to the point of a good decision is the hallmark of a great board.

Too many boards deal themselves, or allow themselves to be dealt, out of the action. The burden is on boards to demonstrate that they can add value to a process that could be, and, in too many cases is, happening without them. Good boards have good meetings where they make good decisions, based on well-gathered and presented facts.

Meetings, it is important to remember, are not an end in themselves. Boards do not exist to meet. Meetings are the means to an end, and that end is to deliver on the identified mission.

CHAPTER 13

A Strategic Agenda

The most common complaint I hear from boards is that they don't have enough meeting time to cover their agenda. "If we only had more time!" Well, you don't. And you won't. Time will always be in short supply. It is the one thing we value above money. The issue is not so much time, but agenda—how the limited time is used.

There are only five basic decisions a board needs to make annually.

Many boards—I am tempted to say *most* boards—use their time poorly. They spend time on items which should not appear on the agenda, or they deal with issues that are not presented in the most helpful way. Boards can easily get into a counterproductive routine.

Instead of going through the usual minutes, reports, old business, new business, big business, and adjourn routine, why not wipe the slate clean and approach the agenda strategically? Allow me to suggest that there are only five basic decisions a board needs to make annually, and some may need only to be revised and reviewed annually.

1. **The Strategic Plan.** This is your opportunity to invent the future you want for your organization. The board should prepare this in two parts:

    The short form. One sentence. Using Habitat for Humanity as an illustration: "Building houses for God's people in need."

    The long form. Perhaps a page-long elaboration of the practical values inherent in your mission. Again, using Habitat as an example:

    - Simple, low-cost houses.
    - Homeowner participation through sweat equity.
    - Use of volunteers.
    - Tithe income to sponsor houses overseas.
    - Increase public awareness of the need for housing.

    This strategic plan should be reviewed annually. It might, or might not, change every year.

2. **The Annual Plan.** "This year we will…" State the plan as outcomes, not activities. The Annual Plan is drawn from or built on the Strategic Plan. The Annual Plan outlines *how* the purpose will be achieved and *who* is responsible to see that that happens (usually known as delegating). Drawing again on Habitat to illustrate:

    - Increase the number of families served by building a stated number of houses.
    - Devise a strategy to insure the availability of lots on which to build.
    - Devise a strategy to increase our volunteer corps.
    - Reduce our monthly homeowner-mortgage payment delinquency to a stated amount.
    - Test a plan whereby paid-up homeowners accept the challenge of building a house for another deserving family.

3. **Appoint, evaluate and "direct" the CEO.** S/he is the person on whom you rely to fulfill the organization's goals. Does your executive have the right competencies to accomplish what you expect?

Is s/he focused on the same priorities and is s/he able to achieve them by working through others?

Deal clearly with questions of compensation, tenure, additional training needed, and so on. Take good care of your executive. S/he is the franchise player who wins the game.

4. **The budget.** This is the instrument by which an organization distributes its limited funds. It enables the strategic goals to be realized. Boards too easily fall into the "Increase/Decrease everything by 5%" syndrome. Every few years a board should go back to zero-based budgeting. Every activity must demonstrate that it is contributing to the strategic goal.

Budgeting right is not easy. Some budgets are too detailed; some too scant.

The challenge is to make the dollars work. There should be no "walking around" money. Every dollar should be directed toward an objective. Nonprofits have much to learn from the for-profit sector when it comes to getting the maximum bang for the buck.

5. **The policy manual.** This is the medium through which the board conveys to management how things are to be done. Policies grow out of experience. Some policies are task-oriented, while others concentrate on values the board wants to uphold and preserve. A few areas the manual should cover are:

- Procedures for financial management.
- Employee personnel standards/qualifications.
- Criteria for… (issues that recur frequently).
- Grievance procedure.
- Employee-performance appraisal.
- Compensation and benefits.
- And on and on—as needed.

If board work can be reduced to such basics, why are boards so busy? Granted, I have simplified considerably here, but my point is to get down to basics. Try making this strategic-agenda approach your starting point, and then add as needed, but keep it simple and basic. Keep it strategic and focused on governance—above the line.

A board sets the standard for the entire organization by how it conducts its business.

Boards that are focused, forward-looking, strategic, and yet congenial in how they conduct business, can expect these traits to be replicated throughout the entire organization.

Good board work is predicated on good meetings. Good meetings are predicated on strategic agendas.

CHAPTER 14

Planning Effective Meetings

Planning an effective meeting begins immediately after the preceding meeting adjourns. That is the best time to identify issues that need to be addressed and to make assignments. The next meeting can build on the previous one. This practice also avoids discontinuity so characteristic of nonprofit boards whose directors have many other preoccupations.

The agenda makes assignments and identifies what will be discussed in what order and how meeting time will be distributed. A good agenda does not guarantee a good meeting, but good meetings are not likely to happen with a poor agenda or the wrong agenda.

Who draws up the agenda?

The Chair and the CEO do it together. If the Chair is responsible for how the board functions, as I advocate, it follows logically that the Chair should participate in agenda preparation. It is equally logical that the CEO should participate, since the CEO is closest to the program, which is where many board issues originate. In practice, CEOs commonly produce the first draft, allowing the Chair to review it and make changes if s/he wishes before it is distributed.

How is the agenda arranged?

Does reporting appear early or late on the agenda? Theoretically, I favor early, because reporting provides background against which subsequent decisions are made. A board should not be asked to support a program expansion, only to learn later in the meeting that income is down, or that there have been unexpected expenses.

Conversely, when reporting appears early on the agenda, it often ends up taking a disproportionate amount of time. Unless discipline is practiced, boards find themselves attending to the urgent while neglecting the important.

My preference on balance is to schedule reporting early in the agenda with three procedural conditions. First, reports must be distributed and read in advance of the meeting. Time spent discussing those reports must be restricted. Second, general reporting should be separated from action proposals, which should appear as agenda items later in the meeting. Third, I recommend adoption of a *consent agenda*, in which housekeeping issues like minutes and reports are approved by consent and without discussion, unless a director requests otherwise.

It is customary and preferable to address unfinished business before new business.

Good meeting planning involves time management, since time is always limited. The agenda should include a suggested time allotment for each category of reporting or discussion, if not, in fact, each agenda item. This helps presenters plan their presentation within the designated amount of time. It also permits everyone in the room to track how the meeting is progressing and to gauge how much airtime they should use.

An experienced Chair does not cut off a lively and relevant discussion merely because the preassigned time has expired. The Chair may call attention to the time, thereby reminding participants to gauge their comments accordingly. There are always items that run over, and some that resolve more quickly. In the end, the agreed-upon adjournment time should, as a matter of rule, be adhered to. Skillful Chairs protect the bottom of the agenda and move the discussion along without appearing to be hurried or heavy-handed.

Agenda ready?

Only items that have been properly processed and which are ready for board action should be placed on the agenda. Inexperienced or incompetent CEOs or committee chairs should not be allowed to escape responsibility by placing on the board agenda sticky items that are within their responsibility to execute. Doing so is a disservice both to the board and to the CEO and leads to bad decision-making. I am fond of saying, No raw meat! If someone—staff or committee—serves you raw meat, send it back to the kitchen.

> **No raw meat! If someone—staff or committee— serves you raw meat, send it back to the kitchen.**

The role of the Chair

The Chair is responsible to keep a discussion focused and moving toward a consensus. This goes better when the Chair is not directly involved in making presentations or overly insistent on getting his/her way. The Chair's part in conducting meetings is critically important.

I was chairing the Habitat board when it was debating the purchase and renovation of a new headquarters building. The debate had gone on for most of an hour—pro and con, back and forth—when it dawned on me that I might be called on to break a tie vote. I concluded that if it came down to a tie vote, although I was for the proposal, I would vote against it on the grounds that a vote of such importance should not pass by a single vote.

Remember that the Chair is obligated to hear and respect, but not necessarily agree with, everyone's point of view. The servant Chair at points surrenders regular board prerogatives in order to be evenhanded and to give voice to all points of view.

Let it not be said of you, as the Apostle Paul said to the Corinthians, "Your meetings do more harm than good." The quality of a board's meetings is a measure of the board's effectiveness. Good organizations have good meetings. Good meetings are a prerequisite for greatness.

CHAPTER 15

Whose Rules of Order?

A ll public discourse is governed by rules, but rules must be adapted to the setting. An assembly of several hundred people working together needs different rules than a small committee.

More than 100 years ago, General Henry M. Robert wrote a book on parliamentary law known as *Robert's Rules of Order*. It is based on rules used in the British Parliament, adapted for use by the U. S. Congress. It has become the universally accepted procedure by which meetings are conducted.

Robert's Rules provide for an orderly, democratic process. They are predicated on the principles that **A.**) the majority has the right to decide, **B.**) the minority has a right to be heard, and **C.**) rights of absentees need to be protected. The 75th-anniversary revised edition lists 44 motions and sets forth the use and functions of each.

With due respect for this revered authority, and while affirming the need for order, my conclusion is that *Robert's Rules* are more appropriate in the U.S. Congress, with 435 eager congresspersons competing for limited air time, or in large assemblies rather than in nonprofit committees or board meetings. In a less formal setting, *Robert's Rules* are more likely to manipulate than to facilitate, to intimidate than to empower. In a small setting, they make me feel like David in Goliath's armor.

A good meeting is one in which the members are free to address the issues and arrive at conclusions together. A synergistic effect emerges which transcends the wisdom contributed by any one member, or even the sum of the members. The strict enforcement of *Robert's* distracts from this kind of spontaneity.

> **In a less formal setting, *Robert's Rules* are more likely to manipulate than to facilitate, to intimidate than to empower.**

Robert's has its place. There must be order. But for smaller, more informal settings, my preference is to minimize legalism; to be informed by *Robert's*, but to regard it as the German proverb suggests: "A soup that is not to be eaten as hot as it is cooked." The higher and more appropriate goal is to create an atmosphere where spontaneous but disciplined participation happens.

My own experience in conducting meetings pushes me toward more informality, while, however, always seeking to uphold *Robert's* principles. Instead of going through the usual call for motion, second, and question, when discussion has progressed sufficiently, I announce, "I am testing mutual consent." If there is no objection, the issue is considered to be resolved. If there is objection, discussion continues to the point of consent, or, if that is not possible within a reasonable time perimeter, I ask that discussion be tabled.

I am intrigued by a variation of this practice used by the Mennonite World Conference General Council, an international multilingual body of about 150 members. Each participant is issued an orange and a blue card. When a member feels there has been sufficient discussion, s/he raises the orange card suggesting readiness to vote. When a significant amount of orange appears, the Chair calls for the vote, moving the discussion along while holding to democratic principles.

It is good to be reminded that, while in our system "majority rules," majorities are not always right. The Bible, in fact, likens the majority to the broad road that leads to destruction! And while the majority has its way, it still needs the support of the minority to make it work. Consensus is the ideal, but it is not always possible.

The test of a good meeting is not whether you conformed to the *letter* of *Robert's Rules*. I am more inclined to consider Jesus' rules of love and justice. Were the three principles undergirding *Robert's*, as summarized in paragraph three above, complied with? Was there an open, trusting atmosphere where members expressed themselves freely and respectfully? Were good decisions made? Do the decisions represent all who were present, and do they own them?

When I transferred the position of Chair of Habitat for Humanity International to my successor, I did not give him a gavel with which to rule someone out of order, but a towel suggesting servanthood. I did not give him *Robert's Rules of Order*, but a Bible, opened to I Corinthians 13, the well-known New Testament love chapter.

CHAPTER 16

Bad Habits Great Boards Overcome

Meetings, a cynic has said, is where you keep minutes and lose hours. I have seen meetings like that; I've participated in more than a few, in fact.

Boards get into a routine. Stated pejoratively, they get into a rut. After a time, they are convinced that there is no other way to operate, even though their meetings fall far short of the best practices. Were it possible to MRI your meetings as a hospital MRIs your knee, what pathologies would it reveal? Here are seven all-too-common practices that great boards seek to eliminate.

1. **Drawn-out and inconclusive meetings.** Either business is not well presented, or your board does not know how to process what is presented. Or maybe your board is busy doing below-the-line management work.

   Whatever the reason, meetings should not be allowed to run on endlessly. Well drillers, it is said, are expected to strike water in a reasonable time or to stop boring. In a weak moment I once said at a church meeting that the Holy Spirit leaves between 9:30 and 10:00 p.m. We can go on meeting, but little will be accomplished.

2. **Poor attendance and habitually late starting times.** An unexcused absence is not neutral. It is negative. At Habitat International our rule was two unexcused absences and you're out. We retired a director of national prominence by enforcing this rule.

Tardiness suggests a lack of discipline. It implies that your meetings are not important. It wastes the time of those who arrive on time. Punctuality, both starting and adjourning, should be the expectation. I have started calling meetings a minute before the hour, that is, at 12:59 p.m., to signal that the meeting is expected to start promptly at 1:00.

3. **Few decisions.** These boards' meetings consist mostly of receiving reports, followed by free-flowing undirected discussion, leaving little or no time for new business. Stop giving priority time to the past (reporting is by definition "past"), lighten up on the present, and give your best attention to the future. The *future* is the board's domain.

Some boards go to great lengths to duck hard issues, mumbling under their breaths, Thought this is what we have staff for. A board is known by the decisions it makes.

4. **Little discussion, or discussions dominated by a few.** Many boards are dominated by a few, while other members are intimidated and prefer to stay out of the crossfire. Either people have nothing to say (that's worrisome), or with a shrug of the shoulder they imply, What's the use? It doesn't matter! I would rather contend with a raucous meeting where passions rage, than one where everything appears to be scripted and members are afraid to express themselves.

Here's an object lesson from tea-making which I learned in Germany, where serving tea is an art form. If the tea bag is removed as soon as the water has reached a certain color, the cup of tea has benefited only from the fast-releasing ingredients. The richer, deeper flavor comes when the finer and slower-releasing ingredients are permitted to emerge. The same is true also of board meeting discussions, at least after a reasonable amount of time.

5.   **Automatic reelection of incumbents, as well as noncontributing members with poor attendance records.** Failure to deal with substandard director performance makes it the norm for all board members and precludes the board's leap to greatness. Directors are not elected for life. That chair is yours for a time; then it will be assigned to someone else. You have a limited time within which to make your contribution; then it's over and you're out.

6.   **Organizations with many secrets.** Executive sessions have their place, but when a board becomes overly secretive, or when the same information is not available to all directors, it is a troublesome sign. I prefer to deal in an open room where trust is in evidence and deserved. Executive sessions should be restricted to matters of personal confidentiality or to major developments that are not ready for public consumption.

> **When a board becomes overly secretive it is a troublesome sign.**

Directors should not be permitted to say in private what they are unwilling to own up to with the full board.

7.   **An agenda loaded with problems without proposed solutions.** I like a motto I saw on a desk in Colombia: *No Presente Problema, Soluciones.* Identifying a problem is only half a presentation. The other half is to suggest a solution for the board to test.

When a board allows itself to be maneuvered into spending time on issues that are not appropriately pre-processed, it is using its time poorly, meetings are unnecessarily long, and decisions are likely to be poor. Great boards are always willing to address problems. They spurn hand-wringing. Their search is directed toward solutions.

These counterproductive habits need to be stopped and can be stopped. But changing corporate culture and practice takes discipline and resolve. The ruts get deep.

Better board meetings result in better decisions, better utilization of time, and greater organizational effectiveness. Improvements made at the board level are also observed by staff, resulting in better staff meetings. Boards set the example for the entire organization.

(See Exhibit F., Writing Effective Proposals for Board Action.)

CHAPTER 17

The Role of the Chair

The Chair—a nondescript title for an important office. Chairing is commonly thought to be synonymous with "presiding." Presiding is an important function assigned to the Chairperson, but the role of the Chair is broader. The Chair's role is one of the least prescribed of any within most organizations. A Chair, it has been said, must be able to write on a blank sheet of paper. While the Chair has considerable freedom to define the office, it should be clear that the office of Chair is not a fit for everyone. An ideal Chair is servant of all.

The Chair's non-meeting role

The Chair's not-in-session function, though less public, is probably as important as the Chair's presiding over meetings.

It requires the Chair and CEO to be in good communication. When

> **The Chair represents the board when it is not in session.**

I chaired the Habitat International board, I met with the CEO and persons who reported directly to him between our three-times-a-year board meetings. We were in contact additionally by telephone and email as necessary.

The Chair represents the board when it is not in session. The Chair serves as the CEO's supervisor, or point of reference, and as the board's spokesperson, taking care not to usurp the role of the board and to keep it well informed.

The Chair also appoints standing committees and helps to coordinate their activities. Much business comes to the board through its committees. Unless committees are supervised, they can take on a life of their own. They sometimes bump into each other, run over staff, or get into the CEO's hair. The Chair must keep that from happening.

Pre-Meeting role

As I've already suggested, the Chair participates in drawing up the board-meeting agenda. Meeting planning should begin immediately after the preceding meeting has adjourned. It may, in fact, grow out of it. Assignments are made, usually in consultation with the CEO, either to staff or to a committee.

The agenda identifies what the board will discuss, and who is responsible and how much time is allotted for each item. The agenda should be released days in advance of a meeting, together with the board docket.

The CEO often prepares the first draft, but the Chair should review it before its release to the board. In so doing, the Chair exercises judgment over whether an item belongs on the board agenda and if it is ready to be processed there. Issues not adequately pre-cooked should not be permitted. Unless discipline is practiced, a board will find itself very busy with all the wrong stuff.

The role of the Chair in presiding

The Chair is the host, making everyone feel comfortable and welcome. The Chair is the master of ceremonies, keeping the program focused. The Chair is the timekeeper, attempting to distribute the limited time available across the whole agenda. Sometimes when chairing a meeting, I feel like an auctioneer seeking the highest bid. The board sometimes feels like a jury.

The ultimate test of a Chair is not whether a meeting adjourns on time, although that is important. The ultimate test is whether the Chair was able to lead without being heavy-handed and by involving the whole board in making wise decisions, while also dismissing the meeting on schedule.

Discussion should not be permitted to go on indefinitely.

I was once criticized by a board member for sneaking a look at my watch while a prolonged discussion was underway. It seemed distracting to her, perhaps intimidating. My first reaction was to cry, Cheap shot! After all, you expect me to adjourn the meeting on time. Then a better thought occurred to me. Sure, I need to keep track of time, but I can do it less conspicuously. Thereafter I placed my watch on the table so I could check it without being noticed. (And I never shook my watch to see if it had stopped!)

The role of the Chair is to lead the board to a consensus. It often happens that while processing one issue, a second issue is introduced. The two chase each other around on the board table like two playful puppies with little more result. The effective Chair separates the two, suggesting which one is now under discussion, and how and when the second issue will be addressed.

If discussion is prolonged, I may remind the board of the hour and what still remains on the agenda. I may also suggest that tabling may be an option. Discussion should not be permitted to go on indefinitely.

A reminder to Chairs

You are the Chair, not royalty. You, too, are accountable—to the board and to the members. As so poignantly stated by Robert Greenleaf, "No one, absolutely no one, is entrusted with the operational use of power without the oversight of the fully functioning trustees."

President Lyndon Johnson, not the humblest of men, said upon leaving office, "The Presidency has made everyone who occupied it, no matter how small, bigger than he was, and no matter how big, not big enough for its demands." That puts chairing into perspective.

Chairs, you are expected to lead, not dominate.

So Chairs, you are expected to lead, not dominate. You are expected to hear everyone, whether you agree with him/her or not. You should persist in helping the group find a way, not insist that things be done your way. It is good to look over your shoulder occasionally to see whom, if anyone, is following!

CHAPTER 18

The Role of Recording

Recording secretary is one of the least desired positions on any board or committee. Yet it is one of the most important. If the agenda contains what will come before a board when meeting, the minutes record for posterity what transpired.

The approval of minutes is often done so perfunctorily that it leaves the impression that minutes are a mere formality; some might even say a nuisance. Not so!

Minutes have four functions:

1. **Legal:** The first thing a lawyer requests in a legal proceeding is the minute book.

2. **Authorization:** Minutes are the official basis by which an activity is authorized.

3. **Informational:** Minutes provide information about what transpired in a meeting for the benefit of absentee members and others with a right to know.

4. **Historical record:** Minutes preserve what was done for future examination.

Minutes should be written with these four functions in mind.

Who records the minutes?

This task is usually assigned in the bylaws to the Secretary. In practice, at least in corporations with a professional staff, minute-taking is often assigned to a staff person. This frees the Secretary to participate in board deliberation, but it also leaves me with a little disquietude. Think about it. Is it wise to assign this important above-the-line responsibility to a below-the-line person? Delegating in this way cedes to a staff person the authority to choose the language by which a board action will be implemented.

> **A meeting is not completed until the minutes are written and approved.**

Ultimately, I will not object if the minutes are *approved* by the Secretary before they are released—and not merely as a formality. Asking a staff person to record the minutes does not change the fact that the Secretary is legally responsible for the minute record.

Desired length?

Some minutes are, in my opinion, too detailed, while others are too brief.

I note that minutes tend to be longer when recorded on a lap-top, and I am not always sure that is good. People are inclined to take minutes for granted in any case, and, when they are too detailed, the temptation is to ignore them altogether. The needle has a way of getting lost in the haystack.

My practice, and I have written many minutes, is to make extensive use of attachments. Attachments have a double advantage. First, they shorten the body of the minutes by not needing to re-state details that are included in the attachment. Second, they increase authenticity. The original document goes forward for future examination, rather than a second-hand summary.

In the distribution of minutes, attachments are included only for the official minute book and for persons not in attendance, since those who attended already have them.

Minute approval

Some organizations have the practice of submitting a draft of the minutes to the board Chair before releasing them to the full board. That is appropriate, if it does not result in undue delay. Finally, it is important to remember that minutes are official only after they are approved by the board at its next meeting.

Timing

Minutes, I feel strongly, must be available within a matter of days following a meeting, at least in draft form. This is especially true for boards that meet monthly or more frequently. Minutes are never easier to write than immediately after a meeting. How else is management, or anyone else, to know how a complex issue was officially resolved so that they can proceed with implementation?

The value of a meeting is diminished appreciatively by carelessly recorded minutes and by a long delay in circulating the minutes.

Freedom to interpret?

Minutes must be the complete, true, and accurate record of what transpired at a meeting. I do not like minutes to have a lot of verbatim, "He said ... she said," but they should record the main points that entered into a conclusion.

A good Recording Secretary can make a chaotic meeting look more orderly than it was (the opposite is also true!), but a Secretary is *never* entitled to change the meaning of what transpired.

Careless chairing makes minute-taking difficult.

Written proposals

Minutes are easier to write when major issues are presented in proposal form, complete with an actionable recommendation that states the action being requested. (For a model, see Exhibit F., Writing Effective Proposals for Board Action.) This permits a discussion to be directed to the recommendation, with accompanying materials serving as background. This kind of form greatly facilitates recording the meeting and increases accuracy. (I consider it a coup when a recommendation I write is found to be so appropriate that it is approved and read right into the minutes.)

Boards like to work with proposals because it saves meeting time, it focuses the discussion, and it results in better decisions. Management likes proposals because they allow the person making the recommendation to, in effect, write the enabling minute. But a board is never obligated to give its carte blanche approval to a recommendation. It is free to amend and even disapprove as it sees fit.

A meeting is not completed until the minutes are written and approved. They are the official record of what transpired.

CHAPTER 19

Great Boards Have a Good Fight—Occasionally

I can think of few things more boring and useless than a board on which everyone is always in full and complete agreement. I mean, what's the use? Either there is nothing on the agenda worth differing about, or nobody cares, or what is passing for a board is actually a rubber stamp.

When one former Chair of Mennonite Central Committee conveyed the Chair to his successor, he observed that during his 33 eventful years, all actions had been unanimous. Unanimous? I learned later that when there was a split vote, he called for a second vote in which the dissenter was expected to acquiesce and apparently always did.

Is that good or bad?

Board dynamics have within them the pressure to conform. This pressure can be so strong that it may call into question the loyalty, or even usefulness, of a dissenter. Independence of thought is not only discouraged, it is penalized. The unspoken expectation is to *conform!* In the sad Watergate saga the understanding was "To get along, you go along."

I have never observed this, but I am told that when sheep are released from a corral through a narrow pass, if the first two or three are required to jump over a stick, the rest jump, even after the stick has been removed. How like sheep some boards are, all jumping in unison to the leader's command.

There is a tendency to believe that decisions arrived at by a group process must be accepted unquestioningly. "We can't all be wrong!" If only that were true. I recall more instances than I have fingers when a unanimous decision, democratically arrived at, was dead wrong and had to be redone. In a spirited argument with my MCC boss, I used as my clinching argument, "I am authorized by the committee to do this." His quick retort, "You are not authorized to be stupid!" How right he was. (We did not take the action under consideration.)

I was invited to address a church body in western Canada. Before my turn came, they reported on a controversial issue which they had spent considerable time processing. Before announcing the final vote, the Chair, knowing that it was not unanimous, reminded the body that there is no guarantee that a majority is right. While holding his audience in suspense, he reminded them that in the Bible the majority is pictured as being wrong. It is the broad road that leads to destruction while the narrow road leads to life eternal. Richard Nixon won the popular vote by a landslide before he was driven from office in disgrace.

For everything there is a season, and so also for dissent. Unless you are a stubborn contrarian, dissent probably does not come easily. I do not enjoy dissenting, but sometimes it is necessary. In one meeting I felt compelled to cast three lone negative votes. I felt vindicated when two of those items were later presented for reconsideration.

Dissent must be learned. Anyone can be contrary. Finding the underside of an idea does not take great skill. To be able to evaluate the worth of an idea, and then to articulate your position in such a way as to be understood and respected by others in the room, requires a high level of self-differentiation. Great directors have the capacity to express themselves while remaining in touch with their peers.

The burden is not entirely on the dissenter. Great boardrooms are characterized by a depth of relationship and a level of trust that permits dissent. Open debate and independence of thought are welcome.

When chairing, I never ask dissenters to change their vote to make an action unanimous. Frankly, I admire anyone who has the intellectual capacity to arrive at a conclusion independently. Dissent serves notice that there is a point of view that has not been factored in to everyone's satisfaction. It may yet merit attention when all is said and done.

Dissent must be learned. Anyone can be contrary.

The final test of dissenters is how they conduct themselves after their minority status has been determined. A helpful model comes to us from a friend in Oklahoma who was one of seven men shingling the addition to a church building. It was a miserable day, and the turnout was disappointing. During a break one shingler volunteered, "And I did not even vote for this addition." It turned out that none of them had voted for it, but they were there shingling it.

As there is good and bad cholesterol, there are good and bad fights. Bad fights result from a clash of egos, each seeking its own way. Good fights may erupt occasionally as dedicated and independently minded directors seek the best ways to further their mission, and then move ahead with a united front.

DISCUSSION QUESTIONS

1. Assess the quality of your board/committee meetings:

KEY

5	4	3	2	1
High				Low

- Attendance   5 4 3 2 1
- Meeting preparation (quality of docket)   5 4 3 2 1
- Leadership of the meetings   5 4 3 2 1
- Clarity of the assignments   5 4 3 2 1
- Utilization/distribution of meeting time   5 4 3 2 1
- Completeness and accuracy of the minutes   5 4 3 2 1
- How well are you fulfilling the purpose for which you exist?   5 4 3 2 1
- Overall rating   5 4 3 2 1

List areas for improvement _____

_____

_____

2. Is there a time on your annual calendar when you put other business aside and evaluate the quality of your meetings and make resolutions for improvement?

3. Review your minute book. Are you making decisions? If so, are they good decisions?

4. Do the staff and board committees present their reports and recommendations in ways that make it easy for board members to know what action is expected?

5. How well is the board able to process an issue to a wise conclusion? Are discussion and debate permitted, maybe even encouraged, or are you mostly expected to approve what is presented?

6. How do you describe your meeting atmosphere? Trusting, tense, business-like, raucous, orderly, spontaneous, creative?

7. Are you supplied with a board docket, including an agenda, sufficiently in advance? Is there evidence that board members study the docket before the meeting?

8. Does your board have dissent? If so, how well do your board and its leadership manage it?

9. Does your committee or board have some bad habits that interfere with effectiveness? If so, name them and suggest ways to purge them.

_____

_____

_____

PART IV

Great Boards Evaluate Performance

E valuation is one of the most neglected of board tasks. This is unfortunate because evaluation is an essential part of accountability and self-improvement. Without evaluation, a board is unable to know if its efforts are, in fact, doing any good.

I was present when a nonprofit board was contemplating the approval of a multi-million-dollar budget without even once asking what was accomplished with the millions that had been appropriated the year before. Why are boards so negligent about evaluation?

"A board has a right and a need to
answer two questions in depth:
1.) Activities: Were the board-approved
plans carried out?
2.) Outcomes: Did they have the
desired effect?"

−page 99

CHAPTER 20

Great Boards Evaluate Themselves

"The last thing a board will evaluate is itself," stated a critic with scathing accuracy. Talk about evaluating the CEO, and some directors roll up their sleeves. Talk about evaluating the board, and they ask with a quizzical look, Us? Why? I thought we were in charge.

I can identify five reasons for this unfortunate neglect.

1.   **Many directors assume (incorrectly) that value in is value out:** Everybody is, after all, very busy and we are all so sincere; our effort must surely be worthwhile. Not necessarily. The simple truth is that some things are a waste of time and effort. Some functions are allowed to idle along long after they have outlived their usefulness. Truth be told, for-profit companies are better at ridding themselves of an unproductive activity than are nonprofits.

2.   **Some directors subconsciously fear the results of evaluation.** They would rather not know than to have to face the consequences. Call it the ostrich syndrome.

3.   **Many boards are uncertain about how to evaluate.** Evaluation involves assigning objective value to what is often a subjective activ-

ity. In his little classic, *Good to Great in the Social Sectors*, Jim Collins says, "To throw our hands up and say, But we cannot measure performance in the social sector the way you can in a business, is simply a lack of discipline." Minimally, we can establish a baseline and measure ourselves against our own previous performance. Are we improving?

4.   **Directors may fear the consequences of doing an evaluation poorly.** Rightly so—an evaluation done poorly can do more harm than good. But is that not true of all activity? The better position to take is to learn how to do it better. And we all learn by doing.

5.   **Evaluation is hard work,** and so has never been introduced into the board routine.

The need for self-evaluation is reinforced by the fact that nonprofits are one area of modern life that has escaped heavy regulation. Even journalistic surveillance is spotty and less than rigorous. Many so-called watch-dog agencies use an instrument so faulty, it is as likely to condone inefficiency as to uncover it. The result is that nonprofits may operate mostly in bubbles of their own making.

> **Nonprofits are one area of modern life that has escaped heavy regulation.**

By evaluating itself, a board is accepting accountability to deliver outcomes to its members. It is sending a signal to the whole organization that evaluation is important. Great boards evaluate four things.

1. Board membership

Use Jim Collins' question in *Good to Great*, "Do we have the right persons on the bus?" Are the necessary skills represented? Are all membership categories well represented? Is there reasonable gender balance? Is there a mix of youth and experience? Are there gaps in geographic or denominational representation? Is everyone pulling his or her weight? Maybe most importantly, is there provision for succession, or are we all slated for retirement within a few years?

I served for some years as CEO of a church-related for-profit company. One day it struck me that many board members would be retiring within a few years of each other. I did not want the board to think that I had a hidden agenda to de-select any one of them. So I recommended that the board commit itself to bring one new director onto the board each year for five years, if not to succeed a retiring director, then to enlarge the board. They were a little taken aback. Then they agreed, reluctantly. Before five years had elapsed, we were grateful that our transition planning had not been delayed.

2. Board performance

Great boards ask themselves these questions periodically:

- Are we making significant decisions, or do we mostly approve reports?
- Do we spend enough time proactively addressing the future and preparing for it, or are we mostly living off past laurels and future hopes?
- Are we driven with a passion for excellence in all our doing, or has a mood of complacency set in?
- Do we have the information needed to perform our governance function effectively, or are we operating in the dark?
- Do staff and board committees present their material in ways that respect the ends/means distinction, or do we spend valuable board time sorting out these issues?
- Do we have a collection of basic policies to govern routine activities and to give guidance to staff, or do we keep reinventing the wheel?
- Are our policies filed in a board policy manual and readily available for consultation? Is our manual updated annually, or do we act arbitrarily?

3. Board-meeting effectiveness

Boards should periodically ask themselves these questions about their own effectiveness:

- Is our meeting time well distributed, permitting us to address important and strategic issues, or do we go around in circles until everyone is exhausted, and then adjourn?
- Is the board docket, including agenda and background papers with recommendations, available in advance of a meeting, permitting us to process it thoughtfully? Or do we spend valuable board time listening to reports and trying to understand what action is expected and appropriate?
- Can the soft voices be heard, or are they drowned out by the shrill, and sometimes less reflective, voices?
- Is there an atmosphere of openness and trust, permitting debate and even disagreement in search of the best solution? Or are debate and disagreement seen as disloyal and inappropriate?
- Are our meetings orderly? Do they start and adjourn reasonably on time, or do members drag in late and then ask impatiently, When do we finish?

4. Board organization

Have we created the right offices? Are we served by the right committees? Should some committees be dissolved? Consolidated? Should new ones be added? Do we meet too often? Too infrequently? I am not convinced that the board of an up-and-running nonprofit needs to meet monthly for governance purposes. Most boards that meet monthly are doing significant below-the-line work. That may be necessary for some, but for most, it is likely not governance work.

All of these areas requiring evaluation can be grouped under the overarching questions that are the backdrop to every board's work: Are we meeting our fiduciary responsibility to our members? Are we fulfilling the purpose for which we exist? Are we being good stewards of the trust vested in us by the members, seen or unseen?

A change in how your board works is not likely to come by someone telling you to shape up. Dissatisfied members are more likely to lose interest and walk away. Self-improvement must come from within. Meaningful change occurs when directors, both individually and collectively as a board, say, *Good enough* is not good enough. We can do good *even better.*

When boards refuse or neglect to institute change voluntarily because they are so entrenched or self-satisfied, change is forced upon them, and that is always costly.

Only after a board has made an honest effort to evaluate *itself* is it in a position to evaluate other parts of its responsibility. Only then can it feel that it is discharging its fiduciary responsibility.

(See Exhibit B., Board Self-Evaluation: Board Duties—How Well Are We Accomplishing Them?, and Exhibit C., Board Self-Evaluation: Board Meetings.)

DISCUSSION QUESTIONS

1. Do you set some time aside each year to examine how well you are functioning as a board and to agree on how you might function better? If not, how soon can you put such a review in place? What tools do you need in order to institute this exercise? Who should prepare them?

2. Do you have a succession plan for your officers? If not, how might such a plan be put in place?

3. Do you examine your standing committees each year:
   A. To determine that they are needed?
   B. To insure that they have a focused work plan for the following year?
   C. To insure that they are well coordinated with the CEO and other board committees?

4. If you do not have such a system, how soon can you put such a review in place? What tools do you need in order to institute this? Who should prepare them?

CHAPTER 21

Great Boards Evaluate Program

What is the board's role in evaluating program? You may be think-ing, Doesn't the board approve the program and then delegate staff to implement it? Isn't management, therefore, responsible for program evaluation?

A board's decisions are delegated to management for implementation. It is only reasonable that management should report on its stewardship of that assignment. A board has a right and a need to answer two ques-tions in depth: 1.) Activities: Were the board-approved plans carried out? 2.) Outcomes: Did they have the desired effect? The bottom line for a nonprofit is always, were lives changed?

Evaluation and planning are interrelated. Simply stated, plans must be written so that they can be evaluated. They must have clear objectives, which state the anticipated outcomes. Only then is an evaluation able to determine if the plan was implemented and what it accomplished.

The report which staff brings to the board is usually a summary of the evaluation it prepares for its own administrative purposes, with some recommendations for further discussion. The board should be clear, and even prescriptive, about the information it wants management to include in its report. There is a human tendency to feature successes and to gloss over failures. When a board is superficial or indifferent, it encourages the same by management. Remember that one of the directors' primary challenges is to arrest entropy.

What does the board do with information staff provides?

The board reserves quality time to review a management report both critically and appreciatively. The board allows the report to speak to them and influence future planning. If a board is too superficial, management quickly senses that, and the purpose of management evaluation is undermined. If the board is unfairly harsh, management becomes shy and less forthcoming.

A board should recognize that performance shortfalls may be a result of the plan being overly ambitious, or due to circumstances beyond anyone's control. At its best, planning and evaluation are done in a partnership mode between the board and management. We, not you!

Nonprofits are loathe to think of cost-benefit ratios, but that evaluation cannot be denied. Was an activity cost-effective? It would be a sad program that could not produce some dramatic story of someone helped each year, but at what cost? Is it worth the investment of time and money? Do our well-intended efforts directly benefit people? Is too much being siphoned off through bureaucratic maneuverings that add little to the bottom line?

Those of us on the Habitat For Humanity International board were stunned when one of our number divided the gross program expenditures by the number of houses built, resulting in a much higher cost-per-house figure than anyone had imagined.

What do directors know about program?

Staff may reason, We are the program professionals. True, but not so fast. Management is so close to the trees that it sometimes loses sight of the forest. Management may be living in an illusion it has created to justify itself. Perceptive board members, with knowledge of fewer operating details yet with more objectivity, can cut through self-serving pretense, producing a window of truth.

> **Board members should not allow themselves to be intimidated by what they do not know. They should always seek to learn more.**

Board members should never question whether they have a role in program evaluation. They should not allow themselves to be intimidated by what they do not know, and they should always seek to learn more. It is, after all, through program that directors deliver on member expectations.

Asking good questions is one of the most valuable skills a director can cultivate. An agency I'm familiar with specializes in translating the Bible into native languages. A first-term director noticed that a translation was abandoned unfinished. He asked in all innocence how many such unfinished translations there might be. Management explained in a defensive, condescending tone that it might take most of 20 years to complete a translation. They went on to remind the upstart director that within that span there could be interruptions like illness or national instability. Undaunted, the director respectfully requested to be supplied with a list of uncompleted translations during the past 10 years. The finding surprised everyone. As a result, they accelerated the use of computers and made other adjustments to shorten the time a translation was in process, resulting in an improved completion ratio.

Board members should not allow themselves to be intimidated by what they do not know. They should always seek to learn more, but they should never question whether they have a role in program evaluation.

Preparing to evaluate program

The hardest part is getting started. Here are a few practical suggestions:

1. Write program plans with measurable goals in mind. Create a plan to evaluate against.
2. Arrive at an understanding with management about what the board will expect at year-end so that the board can evaluate program.
3. Complete the cycle by allowing the evaluation to inform the annual program and budget planning.
4. Do it! You may need several annual cycles before you settle into a helpful routine, but soon you will ask, Why did we wait so long?

Member expectations are fulfilled through program. Program is continually shaped by evaluation.

By perceptively analyzing the past, we learn better how to plan for the future. Evaluation is, therefore, an essential element in increasing nonprofit effectiveness.

DISCUSSION QUESTIONS

1. Does your board set aside some time each year to evaluate how the program is functioning and how it might function better? If not, how soon can you put such a review in place? What tools do you need in order to institute this? Who should prepare them?
2. Are your annual goals and objectives written so that they can be evaluated? What do you need in order to begin doing such an evaluation?
3. Is your annual planning exercise informed by the results of your evaluation? If not, how can you take steps to have that happen?

CHAPTER 22

Great Boards Evaluate Their CEO

The CEO is the only staff person who answers directly to the board. The board sets an example for the whole organization by the thoughtfulness and care it shows its CEO.

Many boards, unfortunately, do not treat their CEOs very well, not because they are mean-spirited, but because they have not given this aspect of their responsibility enough thought. Boards owe their CEOs a clear answer to three questions:

> **No single relationship is more crucial than the relationship a board has with its CEO.**

1. **To whom is the CEO responsible?** The correct answer is, To the board through the Chair. The operative word is *board*, not individual directors. Individual directors may have conversation with the CEO. They may request information or clarification, but it is not appropriate for individual directors to order the CEO around.

If an individual board member has a complaint about the CEO s/he should discuss it with the Chair. There must be a close trusting relationship between the Chair and the CEO. Whenever I have seen tension between a Chair and a CEO, it has been the precursor to serious problems.

2. **Who is responsible to the CEO?** The correct answer is, All employees and volunteers, but in reality it is not always that simple. Board committees complicate the situation. Committee chairs sometimes work closely with staff liaisons, unintentionally bypassing the CEO. Board treasurers and finance committees often have direct contact with the CFO. Precautions must be taken to prevent board committees from undercutting the CEO's authority.

3. **What is the CEO responsible for?** Job descriptions commonly state activities—what the CEO is responsible to *do*. Well and good, but more importantly, especially for the top executive, what is the CEO responsible to *accomplish*? What *outcomes* does the board expect? Too many boards are unclear about what they expect, until they seek reasons to release a CEO.

Board committees can confuse the CEO's task. One of the unhappiest and most tangled relationships I have observed was a board with a series of committees who crisscrossed the CEO's responsibilities. When it all got to be too much, they employed a new CEO without, however, redefining the role of board committees. As a result, the new CEO and board committees again bumped into each other repeatedly, with more than a little bruising and lost motion.

The relationship between board committees and the CEO is so critical and fraught with duplicity that it should be kept under close review by the board Chair.

The CEO evaluation is a good time to examine this. This review should evaluate not only the CEO's performance, but also the web of relationships within which the CEO works.

Who evaluates the CEO?

The Chair is the CEO's supervisor (on behalf of the board) and is, therefore, responsible to conduct the evaluation of the CEO with another board member. There should be provision for input by the entire board and by those staff who report directly to the CEO. The evaluation should be an open process that is not drawn out. I prefer to make it, as much as possible, a two-way *conversation*. The evaluation should consist of two parts:

1. **A face-to-face discussion with the CEO about how well s/he is delivering on the expectations stated in the job description, and how effectively s/he has followed up on the previous evaluation.** How well does the CEO match what will be needed going forward? Should some additional training be considered? Should there be a conversation about career plans or retirement?

    Remember to *hear* the CEO. How does s/he feel about her/his interaction with the board? Take note of actions by the board or individual directors that were helpful or not helpful. Is the board giving enough guidance? Too much? Be sure to invite the CEO to comment on her/his future plans. Challenges. Changes in the near future. A resignation should not come as a surprise when a good supervisory relationship exists.

2. **The evaluation conversation should be summarized in writing and shared first with the CEO, inviting her/him to add her/his own comments.** The report should then be shared with the board in executive session. Finally, the report should be placed in the board file for follow-up.

    This summary should be candid, but as positive as possible without omitting problems and areas where improvement is expected.

Instead of thinking in categories of successes and failures, I prefer the language of affirmations and challenges. The evaluation should leave the CEO feeling energized and clear about expectations.

Evaluation at some level should take place annually. When the relationship is stable and things are running smoothly, a full 360-degree evaluation is not necessary every year. But there should at least be a check-up conversation between the CEO and the board Chair annually.

A board owes its CEO one more thing—thoughtful support. This is not to suggest that the board and the CEO will always agree. They won't and they shouldn't. But even disagreements must take place in the context of respect and support. When trust is lacking, a separation is inevitable.

Salary review is customarily part of an annual review. That is a subject in its own right and an important one, but salary is not the only way a board should express its support and appreciation. Dropping the CEO a note after a particularly trying time or noteworthy accomplishment, or remembering her/him on birthdays or anniversaries, are gestures with good dividends.

No single relationship is more crucial than the relationship a board has with its CEO. A thoughtful annual review is an important part of cultivating that relationship.

(See Exhibit G., CEO Annual Review Outline.)

DISCUSSION QUESTIONS

1. Does your board set some time aside each year to evaluate how it is interfacing with management by way of the CEO? If not, how can you insure that that happens?

2. Does your CEO know what outcomes you expect, and does s/he have the authority and resources to achieve those outcomes? If not, how can you insure that that happens?

3. Does your board care for its CEO? Does s/he feel supported or taken for granted? Does an atmosphere of teamwork prevail? What method do you have for evaluating that? If not, how can you insure that that happens?

"A good agenda does not guarantee a good meeting, but good meetings are not likely to happen with a poor agenda or the wrong agenda."

−page 67

PART V

More Tools to Increase Board Effectiveness

Better board work, it should be clear by now, is more complex than it appears to be on the surface. There is no simple formula that produces a predictable result. Good board functioning is more like jazz, where you improvise, than it is like a piano sonata, where each note is prescribed. Board service is more art than science.

And yet amid all of this shimmer, there are principles and procedures that point us in the right direction, if not necessarily with precision. ***Doing Good*** **Even** ***Better*** attempts to identify some of these basics, grounded in experience and what I've learned from others.

Sometimes against our better judgment we persist in the old when reason argues for the new. We know what we should be doing but we do not always do it. We have a proclivity to procrastinate.

Board service presents us with challenges that may call for behavior and approaches beyond what we find comfortable. I like to see these as opportunities for personal growth and for greater balance and effectiveness in boardmanship

As much as possible, enter board service with an inquiring mind, always seeking to find ways of doing good *even* better.

"Crises are not something we deal with, and then get on with real living. Crises are part of living."

—page 137

CHAPTER 23

Governing Through Policies

Someone once asked me asked with disarming simplicity, "What is policy?" My reply, formulated on the spot, was, "Policy is instruction to the future based on experience and collective wisdom."

Did you ever wonder why nonprofit directors spend more time in the boardroom than the boards of large corporations, like General Motors, do? Part of the answer is that corporations work by policy, while many nonprofits address each issue on its merit, often doing below-the-line activities that management should be doing. As a venture grows, a board should relinquish the hands-on work it so enjoys and make the transition into policy governance.

John Carver suggests that all board activity should be governed by policy. According to Carver, before a board needs a budget, it needs a policy that regulates budgeting. A board policy on budgeting, for example, clarifies who participates in drawing up the budget and how it gets approved. Many budgets I see either have too much or too little detail. And their formats change each time there is a new treasurer, making comparisons difficult.

Boards that govern by policies are more consistent. They are not prone to more stringency when the treasury is low, or to greater generosity when it is strong.

Boards that govern by policy use their time better. For example, in a new Habitat affiliate, the board is inclined to do everything. As the affiliate grows, so does the agenda and so do meeting length and director fatigue.

So the board appoints a Family Selection Committee (FSC). Now, instead of the whole board sorting through the details, the *committee* processes the applications and recommends families for board approval. Now the board needs only to review the committee's recommendations and deal with exceptions. Policy permits the board to discharge its responsibility without an undue investment of time. The board agenda becomes more manageable, but soon the volume of business coming to the board again exceeds the time available. Other business is neglected. Frustration mounts. It is time for board leadership to determine once again how to deal properly with the items being brought to it.

A policy approach to board governance requires that material be presented to the board in a policy-stated format. The treasurer of a start-up board, for example, suggests a policy that will guide future budget-making, and then presents the budget. The FSC, for example, first recommends family-selection criteria, and then presents the individual families that are being proposed. Initially there is double work, but this policy procedure quickly lightens the board agenda and makes board work more efficient.

Directors pass on to their successors the essence of what they have learned through the policies they leave behind. If you are concerned about organizational perpetuation, review what is in your policy manual.

Given that organizations start without policies, the need for policies becomes more obvious as the organization evolves. The tendency is to resist, to just keep going, to manage time pressures by appointing more committees. The transition to policy governance is a hurdle a nonprofit must overcome in order to make the jump from small to intermediate size and from passable to extraordinary. Failure to do so will result in director fatigue (with a host of unfortunate consequences) and organizational retardation.

Converting to a policy form of governance

A board needs to do the following:

1. Identify the issues that take up a lot of board time.
2. Identify what the board has learned, and the values and procedures you want to pass on to your successors, knowing that they may revise them.
3. Draft a written policy statement that embodies the principles that will guide future actions in targeted areas.
4. Require management and committees to bring not only a specific action they are recommending for approval, but also the underlying written policy that will apply in the future.
5. Initiate a Policy Manual with a user-friendly index, and name someone (the Secretary?) to keep it current. This includes adding new policies and removing policies that have been rescinded or superseded. Retired policies should be archived for historical or legal purposes.
6. Review, amend, and add new polices as suggested by experience.

Instituting this new way of thinking and working will take some time and effort, but it will produce good results.

A qualifier

Having advocated for the role of policies in board governance, I want to offer a word of warning. Everything can be overdone, including policies. Policies should not put an organization on autopilot. Policies need to be revised and, on occasion, suspended. Policies do not replace the human capacity to think and reason, to feel and show compassion, to dream. Policies are intended to serve us, to make our work easier and more efficient. They are servant and not master. Policies belong to us, not we to them.

Governance Through Policies

Buoys to Guide Management

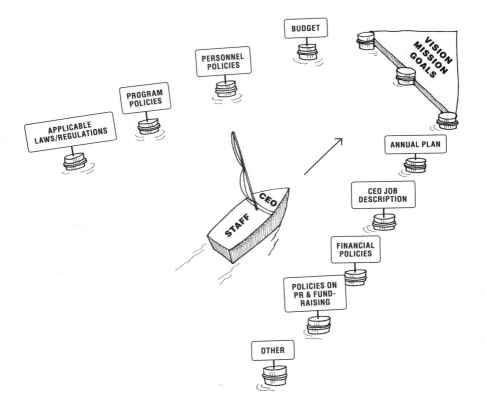

A *policy framework deliniates for management the "territory"*
within which it is authorized to function and what it is expected
to accomplish. The buoys (policies) can be moved or removed
or added to as deemed necessary. They must not be so close as
to frustrate nor so distant (general) that they fail to provide the
needed guidance.

Governing boards are obligated to have a clear understanding with management regarding the board's authority and prerogatives in the day-to-day management of the enterprise. In many cases, these understandings are so vague and undefined that management is left with the impression that it is free to sail the ocean blue.

Too often, clarification comes only after a problem or negligence has occurred, when it is too late to do any good. This results in slippage at the critical juncture where board expectations are converted into program. It also contributes to board/management conflict and not a few terminations. Terminations at this level are always very costly.

This diagram suggests that the first thing a board must be clear on is its destination. What are the expected outcomes?

Next, the board, in consultation with management, lays out buoys (understandings/policies) to guide the captain (CEO). These buoys are part of the guidance system, designed to prevent disorientation in the fog or running aground on shoals, which experience has proven are there. Buoys (policies) are not to box in management, but rather to delineate the territory within which management is free to operate.

If the buoys are too close together, that is, if the policies state the obvious or are too prescriptive, they cause frustration and end up being ignored. If they are too distant, that is, too general or nonexistent, they do not give the CEO the needed guidance.

Buoys can be moved in or out according to experience. A given buoy may be removed altogether when the purpose for which it exists changes or disappears. New buoys can be added as needed. They may even, on rare occasions, be set aside.

Adding or repositioning buoys (policies) should always be done in collaboration between board and management. It should never be done unilaterally or arbitrarily. The objective is to deliver the cargo (program) to the agreed-upon destination, being guided by policies and guidelines based on experience and collective wisdom.

DISCUSSION QUESTIONS

1. How much valuable board time are you spending on issues that could be facilitated better through written and board-approved criteria or policy?

2. Do your written policies adequately state what you have learned and what you expect in selected areas?

3. Would more written policies be helpful?

4. Do you have policies that need to be retired or revised?

5. Are your policies readily available in an indexed Policy Manual?

CHAPTER 24

The Board's Role in Fund-Raising

"**A**ccording to your faith be it onto you," states the Bible. Nonprofits might paraphrase this to say, According to your *fund-raising* be it unto you. The scale of a nonprofit's activity is determined by its ability to raise funds.

Millard Fuller, who raised millions for Habitat for Humanity is fond of quoting another Biblical truism—"Ye have not because ye ask not." When told that Habitat asks too often, he says, "We have tried it both ways. We get more when we ask."

Fund-raising includes many aspects, but it absolutely requires the right people asking the right people in the right way at the right time. What is the role of the board in this important activity?

Every director, particularly directors of young or small organizations, should be involved in fund-raising in one or more of the following ways:

1. **The board of directors devises a plan by which the necessary funds will be raised.** Whether this is by employing salaried fund-raisers, or if it falls to the board itself, a board should have a plan to

raise the money needed to fulfill the budget. This includes making sure that the necessary materials and budget are available to make an effective appeal for funds. Directors should also require that the appeal be consistent with the organization's values and public image.

2. **Directors contribute monetarily in proportion to their means.** An attitude of "I give my time; let others give their money" won't do. Before directors release fund-raisers to solicit contributions on their behalf, they should themselves have contributed. In many organizations, directors contribute or solicit a significant part of the annual budget.

3. **Directors participate in fund-raising by soliciting their friends.** Many dollars are raised as directors ask friends to contribute to their charity, even as they may have contributed to their friends' charities. Call it tit-for-tat, but it works. The challenge is then to cultivate these friends into becoming regular givers.

4. **Directors who are shy about asking, or who are not gifted to do so, should participate in any one or all of the following ways:**
    - By introducing their friends who are potential contributors to the fund-raisers. A database of active and potential donors is as valuable as a bank account.
    - By accompanying other directors or professional fund-raisers who do the asking. The presence of a director speaks volumes to a potential donor.
    - By thanking contributors. It has been said that a contributor has not been thanked until s/he has been thanked five times. Personally, I don't want to be thanked five times. But I firmly believe that donors should be thanked in ways that leave them feeling *appropriately* thanked. That will vary. Some contributors want anonymity while others expect plaques. When people are appropriately thanked, they are more likely to give again, and maybe even increase their gifts. Even timid directors can

enjoy thanking donors. That may be as simply done as making a phone call or sending a thank-you note.

- By volunteering to help with fund-raising events. Remember that this is a volunteer role, not a board role. You are responsible to whomever is in charge, whether board or staff.

A word of caution: Certain understandings should exist before directors are released to each do fund-raising. Precautions must be taken to prevent several directors from converging on a known contributor. Before making a call, a director should have researched the potential contributor's giving record and ability to give. I am not impressed when the newly appointed development director of a charity which I support shows up without having examined my giving record. Amateur fund-raisers frequently find that money which they were seeking has gone elsewhere.

> **Before making a call, research the potential contributor's giving record and ability to give.**

Timing is another important consideration. Donors are less inclined to contribute to a cause that is already past. A new building ceases to have fund-raising appeal once it is completed and occupied. A private school can make an appeal to help students who are unable to pay their tuition, but it is hard to interest donors in covering a deficit that results from unpaid tuition. Executives of nonprofits should constantly be alert for activities that have fund-raising appeal.

Fund-raising is made easier and more effective when it is understood not as begging, but as relationship-building, as inviting persons of compassion to participate in an activity that will better someone's life and, in turn, bless the giver.

When directors (and employees) are directly involved in fund-raising, they develop a more responsible attitude toward the use of money and feel more connected to the givers. I have observed executives who are too far removed from contributors and what motivates them to give.

So, directors, roll up your sleeves and go to work. Find your place in raising the money needed to fund the projects you approve.

DISCUSSION QUESTIONS

1. How are the members of your board involved in fund-raising? Are they as involved as they should be?
2. Are members of your board contributing financially according to their means?
3. Have the directors been coached in the art of friend-fund raising, helping them to be comfortable and effective? If not, how will the board accomplish that?
4. What is the board's plan by which each director has identified his or her personal niche in fund-raising?

CHAPTER 25

The Budget—A Necessary Management Tool

The word budget, I am told, is not in the Bible. Neither is Internet or a host of other current words. A budget is, nevertheless, an essential tool I would not want to be without. Budgets and the process of budgeting do several things:

First, *a budget is a basic planning instrument.* Budgeting *is* financial planning. An organization that does not have a budget is not planning. It is that simple. Budgets help to anticipate how much income is expected from major sources; it likewise anticipates expenses. This makes it possible to foresee if resources will be adequate to complete the plan, or if income will need to be increased or expenses reduced or delayed.

Second, as in some other areas, *the **process** of budgeting is as valuable as the resulting budget.* A budget permits you to examine individual line items and consciously assess each one's merit. Budgeting permits you to compare projected financial activity with previous years, making it possible for you to observe trends. Gross sales/income may be going up, but expenses may be going up faster, resulting in a deficit. Budgeting helps management anticipate trends and make adjustments accordingly.

Third, *the process of budget-building helps the board and management to know if the projected expenditure of money is consistent with their stated priorities and identified mission.* There is always the possibility of saying one thing and doing another—without even knowing it. A careful reading of the budget reveals an organization's true priorities. I can tell much about an organization by reading its budget.

Finally, *a budget is an efficient way of having the board authorize staff to move forward with program.* If an activity is included within an approved budget, it is considered to be authorized. Management needs to explain or seek approval for only those activities that exceed or were not included within the approved budget. This greatly facilitates decision-making by the board and frees it for more productive work.

> **A careful reading of the budget reveals an organization's true priorities.**

In contrast, the manager of an organization that does not have a budget must come to the board for practically all expenditures. This is unnecessarily time-consuming and demeaning to the manager. A budget defines the financial parameters within which the manager is authorized to operate.

How it works

When I was in charge of the Mennonite Central Committee multi-million-dollar overseas program, the annual planning process began by reaching an understanding with the executive committee about how much money would be available for program. Once that figure was established, staff was authorized to distribute the anticipated funds to the respective continental areas according to the agreed-upon program priorities. Then, continental secretaries worked with country directors to draw up their annual program plans within the stated budget.

These plans/budgets then worked their way up though the chain of command (we did not use that term), with final authorization coming from the board in its annual meeting. It was truly a participatory process.

Each of the five levels of administration understood and performed its role within the larger scheme. The ultimate test? It worked. Rapport and trust between board and management was strong. If our plan had a weakness, it was that we did not have a sufficiently defined end goal in mind against which to make our plans.

Arriving at the best procedure and format takes time

One real value of budgeting becomes apparent only after the second or the third year, when meaningful comparisons are possible. Some experimentation may be required before you find the budget format that serves your organization best. When budgets are too detailed, they become cumbersome, making skeptics question if they are worth the bother. When they are too brief, they fail to accomplish their purpose. The challenge is to get started and then adjust as suggested by experience.

One practical tip

I like to work with a spreadsheet that has four columns: 1.) Current year experience; 2.) Current year budget; 3.) Previous year experience; 4.) Recommended budget. In some categories, you might want to include the experience five years earlier, giving you a longer financial history. Much valuable financial information can be condensed on one page using this format.

A confession

My wife and I have never had a family budget. We disciplined ourselves to live within our income, even when we were in Voluntary Service and our income was $10 per month, plus the basics of room and board. So I am not budget-obsessed. However, were I to manage a nonprofit, I would definitely have a budget. All executives should be clear about the authority given to them by their boards and should know where things stand financially as the year progresses.

DISCUSSION QUESTIONS

1. Do your financial reports and annual budgets permit you to project income and expenses, and to track experience throughout the year with comparisons to previous years? Do your full board and management staff understand these tools? Do they use them?

2. What is your board's understanding with management about what management is authorized to do in regard to program and finances?

3. Are the financial reports that the board receives, and the budgeting format your organization uses, giving you sufficient information to make good decisions?

CHAPTER 26

Cautions about Committees

The use of committees has become so universal that to even express
caution may seem sacrilegious, or hopelessly out of touch. When
a board feels overloaded—and don't most?—the reflex is to appoint
another committee. One organization I consulted had 17 committees
and still felt overwhelmed. I suggested the appointment of yet another
committee—a committee to study what committees to eliminate.

Many organizations, including congregations and small or young
organizations, could not exist without committees. Committees are
their engine.

For all the good they do, committees are also the cause of much
confusion and frustration. Let me raise some cautions about the indis-
criminate use of committees and the exaggerated role ascribed to them,
in order to reduce the negatives and improve their performance. First,
three reminders.

1. **Board committees get their assignment from the board
    through a process commonly known as delegation, although it
    is seldom thought of in that way.** Delegation involves authoriz-
    ing one party—in this case, the committee—to act on behalf of
    another—the board.

Delegation is subject to the authority of the delegator. This suggests that committees are subordinate to the board. They are not an end in themselves. They are the *means* to an end, the end being whatever the board has undertaken to do on behalf of the members.

2. **The board's focus is on governance as distinct from management.** Board committees should therefore be focused on *board* work.

    Management may have its own committees, and management may be asked to serve on a board committee, but the focus of a board committee must always be governance—above the line.

3. **The role of board committees needs to be closely coordinated with the CEO's job description.** Unless precautions are taken, board committees, more than the board itself, can easily invade functions that rightfully belong to management.

    Organizations without a CEO (congregations, PTAs, and small or young organizations) often blur the functions of ends (goal-setting) and means (implementation). Once a CEO is in place, the executive function is normally delegated to the CEO, and the board's exclusive focus is governance.

How committee inflation comes about

The organization is young and the directors are inexperienced. They fail to make the above/below-the-line distinction. They do both indiscriminately. As their workload increases, they draw in more people by appointing a committee. Then more committees! And then the committees get enlarged and the meetings get longer, until the signs of burnout are everywhere. Something must give.

> **Board committees have a tendency, if allowed, to take on a life of their own.**

The board appoints a CEO, perhaps part-time at first, and then full-time. But the board committees, though weary, feel committed to what they are doing and continue as before. After a year or so, the CEO is frustrated and the committees are heard to murmur after a long meeting, I'm not sure why we have a CEO—seems we are still doing all the work. Unless precautions are taken, board committees double over management, resulting in inefficiency. This makes for weary directors and frustrated, weak CEOs. In fact, only weak CEOs will tolerate this kind of double-work. Strong CEOs won't put up with it.

Many boards stall precisely at this point. They become focused on distributing their work to committees and lose sight of their primary responsibilities and appropriate ways of working. They should be sharpening their agendas and establishing more policies to apply to routine issues.

More problems with board committees

Board work is meant to be a holistic, integrated process, but committees break it up into numerous entities, some of which are inherently in conflict with each other. For example, a program committee may recommend expansion, while simultaneously the finance committee reports a reduction in contributions. At the same time, human resources may be recommending salary increases. The process bounces around until it finally ends up on the board table.

Board committees have a tendency, if allowed, to take on a life of their own. They assume authority that was never intended, and the board, like a fabled British knight, rides off madly in all directions. Each committee has a piece of the action, and no one sees the whole picture. Board committees can be compared to a series of huge silos which operate under a thin umbrella, the board. Each committee assumes they represent the whole, when, by definition, they represent only a part.

Board committees commonly consume more time than the board itself. They can diminish the role of the CEO and/or the board. They can also distract from the clear accountability that needs to exist between the CEO and the board.

It is commonly thought that committees lighten board agenda, but not necessarily. Unless good practices are followed, committees can complicate and delay the board's decision-making. First, the board defines the assignment. Then the committee does its work and makes a recommendation to the board. The board discusses that and then considers an action. What has developed is a three-step process.

Unless carefully managed, committees and their work can be a very time-consuming, inefficient, and frustrating process. Worse yet, many boards use committees as a way to duck hard issues.

These cautions are real and not simply imagined by some weary curmudgeon. In the next essay we will consider how to avoid these negatives to build on the strengths of committees.

CHAPTER 27

Committees—Getting More with Less

Boards gravitate toward routines. They like to arrive at autopilot where no hard thinking is necessary. When a problem or an issue arises, the reflex is to appoint a committee. If no restraint is exercised, boards cede away most of their functions until they are reduced to doing little more than appointing committees and approving reports.

> **My mantra, No raw meat, applies to committees as well as to boards.**

The cautions I expressed in the preceding essay, and the tendency of boards to assign an exaggerated role to committees, drives me to a minimalist position.

No more committees than necessary

The only committee I consider essential is a Board Service Committee. Its function is to review how the board, committees of the board, and individual directors function. It also vets and nominates officers and directors for election.

Large boards, with a membership that is scattered geographically, may have an executive committee, commonly consisting of the officers.

The executive committee's role should be carefully prescribed so that is does not usurp the board's role. I have serious reservations about the practice of executive committees pre-processing everything before those items reach the board. This practice gives second-class status to directors who are not on the executive committee. It can also lead to double-processing every item.

A finance committee can be useful because it keeps an important area under review. But the committee should not impinge on what the CFO should be doing. The finance committee should be especially alert to the organization's audit process.

Boards that do not have a CEO may appoint working committees to implement board decisions. These may include a fund-raising committee and perhaps others. Board committees must be ever vigilant, however, not to wander into doing staff work and neglect their above-the-line governance responsibility.

I believe that program is so integral to an organization's purpose that it should be the direct responsibility of the board and not of a subcommittee. Human-resources work, for all its importance, usually falls below the line and does not warrant standing-committee status.

There are occasions when special committees are appropriate for a carefully defined function. This includes Task Groups, whose assignment should be outlined in writing, including a sunset clause.

In short, do not look for excuses to appoint a committee. To the contrary, resist doing it. Forming a committee may be a classical case of passing the buck. Do it only after a convincing case for its existence is made.

No larger than necessary

Up to five members is manageable for a committee; seven at the maximum, but the number should never exceed one-third of the board membership. Even a committee of two will do. I once served on a committee of one and enjoyed it immensely! If nonprofits had to pay for committee time, they would use it more sparingly.

Meeting no more often than necessary

Too often too little preparation goes into committee meetings. The result is that many committee meetings are longer and more frequent than necessary. My mantra, No raw meat, applies to committees as well as to boards. Whoever calls a meeting is responsible to insure that the issues on the agenda are ready to be processed by the committee.

Meetings would be shorter if conference rooms had no chairs— guaranteed!

Sometime it is useful to use a strategic approach when planning for a meeting. The person in charge of making a report states what s/he thinks might be a wise conclusion, and then builds the case to support that tentative conclusion. Instead of asking the committee to start from scratch, it has a focal point to begin its deliberation. Such an approach facilitates the meeting and still allows for member participation.

Meeting no longer than necessary

You already know about my 10 p.m. rule—when the Holy Spirit leaves. If a meeting is well planned and presided over, a committee can accomplish in two hours what it's most capable of doing.

In fact, who said meetings must last two hours? You know the old rule—the amount of time required to do something expands to the amount of time allotted. I have had good success with what I call stand-up meetings (giving new meaning to the term *standing commit-tees*) for a one-item agenda. Most of our meeting rooms, I insist, are too comfortable. Meetings would be shorter if conference rooms had no chairs—guaranteed!

Boards also get better results from committees when they require them to produce a job description and an annual work plan. These should identify what issues they plan to address with what anticipated outcomes. Board committees must continually remind themselves of the need to collaborate with the CEO and with other committees to avoid unnecessary conflict and duplication.

Committees do not make policy; the board does. Committees *recommend* policy to the board, and then they are obligated to operate within the board-approved policy. Committees are servant, not master.

Boards get better results when they use committees sparingly and for a defined purpose.

(See Exhibit E., Suggestions for Committees.)

DISCUSSION QUESTIONS

1. List all of your board's active committees. Next to each, state what it is contributing to the board's work; then state whether it is needed. Should any current committees be retired? Should any be combined? Should any new committees be appointed?

2. Do each of your committees have a written job description? Are these descriptions focused on governance issues or on management issues? Does each committee render a written statement of issues it expects to address and with what outcomes?

3. Do committees report their recommendations to the board in actionable form?

4. Is the role of committees clearly delineated from the role of the CEO, or are they frustrating and bumping into each other?

CHAPTER 28

Managing Conflict Constructively

Wherever two or three are gathered ... there will be differences. Take my word for it. Well-intentioned people may look at the same facts and arrive at different conclusions. This need not be bad. Differences exist only when there are multiple options, and that is good. Differences can be a sign of life, of energy. Boardrooms should be greenhouses filled with new life, not graveyards.

The absence of differences may, in fact, be lethargy, indifference, or stifled creativity. Any of these is many times worse than conflict dealt with constructively.

The issue is not differences, but what to do when differences are elevated to the point of conflict. Conflict may be the phase through which some differences pass en route to resolution. But do those differences *pass through*, that is, do they get resolved, or do they become permanently embedded, only to be resurrected in an even more virile form later? It is unquestioningly healthier and potentially more constructive to deal with conflict openly, rather than to deny it, driving it under the table or wishing it away.

When dealing with differences constructively, it is useful to understand the behavioral styles which play themselves out in boardrooms daily:

Competing

Competing directors are intent upon winning—every time. They ignore, deny, or even manipulate facts that do not support their predetermined conclusion. They place a low value on discussion and group process. Their style is individualistic and intimidating. They resort to whatever it takes to prevail.

Accommodating

Accommodating directors support the prevailing point of view. In their eagerness to be liked by everyone, they are quick to agree with whatever solution is emerging, whether it is the best option or not. They invariably agree with the last person who spoke. They always vote with the majority.

Avoiding

Avoiders are uncomfortable with any divergent point of view. Their first objective is not to arrive at the *best* conclusion, but to stay out of the crossfire of anything resembling a disagreement. Even a differing point of view is uncomfortable for them. When the discussion heats up, they shut down.

Compromising

Compromisers are skillful at gathering together points of view on which there appears to be agreement, and then cobbling together their version of a solution. This may appear on the surface to be helpful, but it does not always meet the next-day test. Instead of holding out for the best solution, this approach can pull the discussion to the lowest common denominator.

Collaborating

Collaborators invite alternative points of view. They weigh each on its merit objectively. They willingly risk divergent points of view in their search for the *best* solution. They are not much interested in who wins and who loses. Because collaborators arrive at a conclusion collectively, they also own it collectively and invest in making it work.

The contrarian

Contrarians fix on the underside of an idea, and all ideas have an underside. Locating it does not take much skill or creativity. Whatever is proposed, the contrarian prefers the opposite. If the consensus is black, the contrarian extols white and identifies everything wrong with black.

The first four behaviors listed above are driven by self-interest. How can I win? How can I be liked? How can I avoid being embarrassed? I want to be the hero. By way of comparison, the collaborator's first concern is to arrive at the best solution. His/her strongest motive is to draw the best from the group.

Contrarians are not bothered by being in the minority. They may be disruptive, but even avowed contrarians deserve to be heard. They usually have a point, and, on occasion, they may be right!

Don't deny differences, even conflict, or wish them away.

The challenge that faces every board, and particularly the Chair, is to create a collegial environment where turf and ego considerations are sublimated to seeking the highest common good. This requires trust among the members and a willingness to be vulnerable. It calls for independence of thought and the ability to be differentiated.

I saw this practiced masterfully on one occasion. Two senior church-men had a sharp disagreement. When adjournment time came, one of the disputants asked the other to offer a closing prayer. He rose to the occasion admirably. I don't remember all the words, but the prayer included the memorable line, "Thank you for those who disagree with us. They help us to think thoughts we might not otherwise think." And so they do.

Don't deny differences, even conflict, or wish them away. Embrace the opportunity to find the one option from among several that will serve your organization best.

DISCUSSION QUESTIONS

1. Reflect on how differences are processed on your board. Is the board able to deal with them openly, or are they ignored or driven underground?

2. How is someone who sees things differently regarded? Are such persons valued, or is their usefulness questioned?

3. How skillful is your board in collaborating its way to the best solution?

CHAPTER 29

Working Your Way Through a Crisis

A crisis may be lurking in your future. "The world breaks everyone," said Ernest Hemingway, "and afterward some are strong at the broken places."

Crises usually find us unaware and unprepared and, consequently, uncertain about how to cope. The very qualities that help us succeed are the same ones that make us unsuited for crisis-management. Though there are many kinds of crises, some overarching principles can be helpful:

1. **Crises are a normal part of life.** They are usually under the surface, but their potential for surfacing is ever-present. Crises are not something we deal with, and then get on with real living. Crises are part of living. We are more likely to deal with crises well when we see them in this way, rather than as unwished-for interruptions of the sanguine life we dream about.

2. **"An ounce of prevention is worth a pound of cure."** Often crises confront us with what should have been dealt with long ago. At the root of a crisis is often procrastination. Stated crassly, Keep your house in order.

3. **Sometimes we make an issue into a crisis unnecessarily.** Some issues cannot be solved. Trying to do so may make them worse. We can only live our way through them. The doctor's motto is, Do no harm. Like football players, organizational leaders must learn to play through their injuries.

4. **Prepare for crisis by having a contingency plan in place.** Every organization should maintain a file captioned, "In the Event of a Crisis," with some specific do's and don'ts. Assess ways in which you may be vulnerable. Anticipate what crises may be lurking and devise a tentative recovery plan. For starters, Google "Crisis Management" and spend an hour reading how others have responded to crises. I just read a case study of the crises that confronted Chi-Chi's and Sheetz over food-poisoning resulting from vegetables imported from Mexico. Chi-Chi's did it poorly and is now out of business. Sheetz did it well and did not close a single store.

5. **At the first hint of an impending crisis, a board should do several things simultaneously:**

    - Own it, whatever it is. Do not live in denial and do not hide or run. The facts will be incomplete, and some will be wrong, but the word from the board must be, We are investigating and will report as soon as we have more information.

    - Gather the facts. You will want your own sources, while recognizing that others may know something you don't. Accusations will be everywhere, but stay focused on facts. Find out what really happened. Do not cover up, but at the same time, do not believe everything being said.

    - Establish who speaks for you. That person should be very visible and available, and *everyone* else should be mum. This includes directors, whose only reply should be, "XxxxXxxx speaks for us. I have nothing further to say at this time." The designated spokesperson should give the appearance of being in charge and should be skillful in dealing with the

> **Establish who speaks for you.**

media. (It is preferable, although it is not always possible, that this be the board Chair or the CEO.)

- Be mindful of all the publics that need and deserve to be informed: customers, employees, stockholders or significant donors, maybe legal or regulatory persons. Assume that what is said to one will soon be known to all.
- Establish rapport with the media. Do not succumb to the reflex that believes all reporters are enemies. Work with them toward shaping the news. Help them to *get it right.*
- Accept responsibility. Do not portray yourself as an innocent victim. This may require daily briefings with a level of transparency that will strain you, but any attempt to conceal will immediately become the subject of further investigation. Remember that you cannot manage the media. If treated properly, it can be your ally.
- It is wise to keep one eye on the legal implications, but do not let this become your all-consuming preoccupation. To the contrary, think like the customer, like the public.

6. **Look beyond the crisis.** The public will give you a reasonable amount of time to fix what is broken, but failure to act will be your death knoll. The Chinese word for crisis is composed of two characters—"danger" and "opportunity." When in the 1980s, Tylenol found that its pills had been contaminated, it introduced new safety measures and quickly restored its reputation.

7. **Don't let the crisis get you down or cause you to doubt yourself.** Remember that things are never as good as they appear when they are up, nor as bad as they appear when they are down.

Great organizations are always surrounded by big challenges. They find ways to make stepping-stones out of stumbling blocks. They manage their way through the crises that arise.

DISCUSSION QUESTIONS

1. In what areas is your organization vulnerable that might occasion a crisis?

2. What contingency plan does your board have in place? Whose names and telephone numbers should be readily available in the event of a crisis?

Smelling Salts for Discouraged Organizations

Nonprofits commonly start with a blaze of enthusiasm, but, like people, organizations have a predictable life cycle. Some, like in the biblical parable, show great promise but quickly wither and die. And thousands of nonprofits die each year, but they die hard.

How can an organization be reborn? How do you resuscitate an organization that has gone flat? I have three suggestions, supported by a myriad of real-life examples.

People, people, and people

The bottom line for organizations is always people. People are at the root of organizational decay, as people are at the root of organizational renewal.

> **The people under whose direction a venture went flat are not likely to revive it.**

It is sobering to realize that the people under whose direction a venture went flat are not likely to revive it. As I suggested in the opening chapters (see pages 13-15), before you can get things humming again you must surround yourself with the right people. That action will likely need to be preceded by the even more difficult task of making room for new people with fresh energy and vision.

Great organizations are built around people who have two qualifications: First, those who know something. The world is filled with people of good will, but good will alone isn't enough. A school needs teachers who are qualified to teach, just as a construction company needs people who know construction. Nonprofit organizations need people who know something about running an organization. They need to have proven competencies. What do they know? What can they do?

Second, people with a can-do attitude are needed. As there are introverts and extroverts, right-handers and southpaws, some people are naturally optimistic, while others are inclined to dwell on what won't work. Caution has its place, but you cannot build an organization with nay-sayers. By eternally fixing on obstacles and dangers, pessimists drain energy out of a system. They tip a delicate balance in a negative direction.

I was a partner in a start-up for-profit venture. The concept was exciting, but the devil truly was in the details. Meeting after meeting, we were on the verge of despair. Then good fortune came our way. Our member who had been a successful CFO, and who continually demanded assurances, prematurely resigned. We replaced him with someone whose ideas were rarely well thought through but who was of a can-do nature. Our venture took off. Only in retrospect did we realize the burden of negativism.

Negative people are like dragging brakes. Brakes have their place. I don't want a car without them. But if brakes do not release, they slow things down and eventually they burn out. Do not lose valuable time by trying to get positive results from negative people.

Identify a compelling cause

I was privileged to participate in recruiting and assigning literally thousands of service workers through Mennonite Central Committee.

I learned that strong people are more likely to sign on to a challenging assignment with attending uncertainties, than to one with a maintenance nature.

Be alert to the mistake of presenting your compelling cause in a mundane way. A medical program which highlights its purpose of promoting health will likely evoke more enthusiasm and support than if it is focused primarily on being a business which helps people cope with illness.

Ten Thousand Villages, a fair-trade organization, does not believe it is in the business of peddling unique trinkets, made by poor people in less developed countries, that become conversation pieces in elite circles. Instead, it creates jobs for carvers and basket-makers who are scrimping along on a few dollars a day. MCC's network of ReUzit stores does not exist to dispose of middle-class leftovers and cast-offs. Rather, it is part of an effort that feeds the hungry and restores lives.

If your organization is not throbbing with excitement, pause and consider before you think that the answer lies in a new, multi-colored, glitzy brochure. Look at the needs you are addressing and how you are presenting them to your publics.

Set goals

Put mile-markers in place by which progress can be measured. Some boards are reluctant to set goals for fear of not achieving them. Yet boards that fail to set challenging but attainable goals, complete

> **However modest or ambitious, set an identifiable goal.**

with intermediate markers, have no way of tracking progress. Nothing succeeds like success, it is said, and so it is.

Ventures that refuse to set goals live either with an illusion of progress, or they get discouraged because they have no way of tracking how well they are doing. Whether you measure against the performance of others of like kind, or against your own previous accomplishments, you need some way to see if you are making progress or not.

However modest or ambitious, set an identifiable goal. If you achieve it, don't gloat. Set another goal and get on with it.

Organizational renewal is possible. I have seen it happen. The dead rise, the lame walk, the blind receive sight! It begins with people; people with competencies and can-do spirit. People who set goals for themselves, and then passionately move heaven and earth to fulfill them.

DISCUSSION QUESTIONS

If your nonprofit has lost the spring in its step and is serious about recovering it:

1. Look at who is on the bus, especially at who is in the driver's seat. What steps should be taken to revive the situation?
2. Look at the cause you represent and how you present it. Does your approach make people want to yawn or to quicken their step?
3. Have you reduced what you want to accomplish into a plan with specific goals, including mile-markers to achieve them? If not, how will you do that?

CHAPTER 31

Under the Shadow of Litigation

It seems so contradictory, just so plain wrong, that something as noble as service on a nonprofit board should be subject to personal liability. But such is the case in our litigious society.

It is appropriate that directors of publicly funded nonprofits should be held to a reasonable standard of care. The public needs to be protected against unscrupulous persons who roam the earth and on occasion even infiltrate nonprofit organizations.

Directors and officers should not be paranoid, but neither should they be naïve.

How can directors protect themselves, and the organizations they represent, against legal threats? Directors are, after all, removed from the day-to-day operations. The standard that must be met, and against which director liability is judged, is simply that they exercise a "reasonable standard of care." Consistently abiding by best practices, in both governance and management, goes a long way toward complying with this requirement. Boards are expected to:

1. **Meet regularly, discharge their fiduciary role faithfully, and operate in an open and responsible manner.** If that is not the case, and you are powerless to change the situation, you may consider resigning to escape liability or damage to your reputation.

2. **Mandate management to abide by all applicable laws and regulations, and then monitor to insure that that is happening.** Directors may not understand the fine points of the law, but at a minimum they must not knowingly and recklessly violate laws and regulations.

3. **Require "truth in advertising."** Do not ever purport to be doing what you are, in fact, not doing.

4. **Engage an auditor that is recognized as competent, and insure that the board follows up conscientiously on any recommendations.**

The most common legal transgressions are employment-related. A board is responsible to put in place policies that prevent violations, including these especially vulnerable areas:

1. **Discrimination in hiring and promotion.** Courts and the general public have become very sensitive to matters related to race, gender, or age discrimination. Even apart from the law, matters of discrimination should be of concern to directors. An unproven accusation can be damaging to any organization's reputation.

2. **Sexual harassment.** Directors are expected to instruct management to maintain a safe work environment, including appropriate sexual harassment policies, and then to monitor that the organization is in compliance.

3. **Due diligence in hiring.** For example, an agency that employs someone with a record of sexual harassment without a thorough investigation is liable. Directors may also be held individually liable, unless they can point to an organizational policy specifically requiring management to do such investigations.

Wrongful discharge is the most common source of employment-related litigation, although such charges seldom implicate the board. Directors should require management to show just cause for discharge. This includes documented proof that employees have been given ample opportunity to bring conduct and/or performance up to a reasonable standard. A court is not likely to uphold a discharge if the last review is complimentary or silent on the issue that occasioned the discharge.

Conflict of interest is another vulnerable area. Directors who find themselves with a dual interest—for example, employing a close relative, or leasing a property, or selling something to the nonprofit—should recuse themselves from voting on related issues. Their action should be so recorded in the minutes.

Nonprofits who find themselves in an especially vulnerable position related to a board merger, for example, or with substantial governmental contracts, should exercise extra care about how their actions are documented, including the careful recording of board minutes.

Director liability may also be managed through three procedures that have become common practice:

1. **A bylaw provision that shifts liability from the director personally to the nonprofit, excluding, however, anything of a fraudulent nature.**

2. **A Director and Officers Liability Insurance policy, purchased by the nonprofit, that indemnifies a director or officer against wrongdoing.** D&O policies are subject to limits and retention and apply to both defense and judgments. The defense provision may prove to be more beneficial since most claims are settled out of court.

3. **Some homeowner policies maintained personally by directors also have limited coverage against D&O claims.**

The bottom line in director litigation is contained in what is referred to as *The Business Judgment Rule* which reads as follows:

Even where a corporate action has proven to be unwise or unsuccessful, a director will generally be protected from liability arising therefrom if he or she acted in good faith and in a manner reasonably believed to be in the corporation's best interest, and with independent and informed judgment.

Directors and officers should not be paranoid, but neither should they be naïve. Service on a nonprofit board carries with it the potential of liability, but that liability can be managed by conscientiously and consistently applying the best practices outlined here.

DISCUSSION QUESTIONS

1. As a board member, are you receiving the information needed to exercise a "reasonable standard of care"?
2. Are you aware of practices within your organization that do not meet the "reasonable standard of care" criteria? What is your source of information?
3. Is the nonprofit you serve protecting you with either a bylaw provision, or a standard D&O liability policy, or both? If not, are you prepared to assume that risk, however large or small?

CHAPTER 32

Great Boards Celebrate

Most boards, if rated on a scale of joyfulness, would rank somewhere just above a gathering of morticians. Board work is, to be sure, serious business, but must we be so joyless? Are there no occasions for humor or celebration?

Humor can be a lubricant that relieves tension and helps to focus an issue. I recall a short story told by the then-chair of Mennonite Central Committee about a boy who was banished to his room for refusing to eat a dish of prunes. While standing at his window watching a lightening storm in progress, he was overheard to mutter under his breath, "Such a fuss over a few prunes."

Or this story which Abe Lincoln reportedly told while presiding over a raucous meeting of his Union Army generals. A boy was lost in the woods while a major thunderstorm was in process. In desperation he prayed, "If it is all the same to you, God, I would prefer a little less noise and a little more light."

Humor is different than telling jokes. Humor sees the lighter side of an issue. Sarcasm is not humor. It is biting criticism and feeds negativism, although it may not be entirely pointless. Humor is at its best when it is not caustic or used at the expense of others.

If you are fortunate to have someone in your ranks who can lighten the atmosphere without being obnoxious or too time-consuming, consider yourself fortunate. Humor has its place, even in the boardroom.

Board service should be fun

I can think of few things more deeply rewarding and satisfying than to join with others of like mind to make life better for others. Associating with people of good will is enriching.

Service is pay-back time for many. Our generation has been blessed as few before us and, arguably, like none after us. Mohammed Ali stated poignantly, "Service is the rent we pay for the space we occupy." Service is not a sacrifice. It is a joy that adds meaning to life.

But we enjoy it only when we do it well, when we can see something accomplished, when we see lives changed.

If you are not enjoying your board service, perhaps you should consider releasing your chair to someone who will.

Celebrating

While writing my concluding Chairman's report for the American Leprosy Missions board, I found myself enumerating our accomplishments and concluding each with, "Something to celebrate." Then it struck me. But we never celebrated. I was embarrassed and determined to make up for lost time.

Upon arriving in Greenville the evening before our quarterly meeting, I asked senior staff to help me make room on the agenda for a celebration. They looked at me incredulously. Did I not realize how full the agenda was? "I know, I know—we'll cut the evening session a little short and then we'll celebrate into the night," I said. Looking into their doubtful faces I asked, "What had you planned for our dessert following the evening meal?"

"A cake."

"Excellent. Could we keep that for our celebration? Are there any candles around?"

Diane was softening up and volunteered, "A closet-full left over from a fund-raiser." Then she volunteered to get some balloons and streamers. Chris got into the spirit and offered a favorite celebratory CD. On short notice I asked Carol to emcee the event.

We recessed the evening board session at a record hour. The directors descended the stairs apprehensively. Quickly their mood was transformed by the sound of lively music. Balloons and streamers came into view. For a moment we stood around silently and somewhat awkwardly. Then Carol picked things up with some appropriate remarks, followed by more awkward silence. Clearly, we did not know how to celebrate.

Feeling some obligation to dispel the anxiety, I stepped forward hesitatingly. I selected a candle from the table. Nervously I lit it and, facing the group, I held it high and said, "Here is to the memory of Mike who served us faithfully as treasurer and whose friendship we miss."

The ice had been broken. One after another, the directors and senior staff came forward to light a candle and offer a celebration.

"We must do this again—soon!" We forgot about time as everyone joined in. At the end of the evening, our table of lighted candles looked like an altar, causing some to inquire where the fire extinguisher was located! And then came a virtual chorus, "We must do this again—soon!"

Budget for the event? Maybe $10. The evening ranks among one of the most cost-effective board activities ever!

Celebrate! Look for excuses to celebrate. Celebrate an anniversary, a fund-raising success, a year of accomplishments, a birthday, a retirement, a major staff appointment. It will add a joyful dimension that will make your board's work go better and give you more to celebrate.

DISCUSSION QUESTIONS

1. What can you do to make your meetings be more joyful?
2. When will you have your next celebration?

CHAPTER 33

Leaving Right

"**F**or everything there is a season. A time to be born and a time to die."

A time to engage and a time to disengage, to paraphrase Solomon.

After having invested ourselves in a cause, whether as employees or as directors, we want, and we deserve, to leave with a sense of satisfaction, of being appreciated. Sadly, that does not always happen. Sometimes years of good work are overshadowed by the pain of termination. Instead of feeling appreciated, retirees sometimes end up feeling pushed aside, discarded. Few dynamics are more difficult to manage than those that come when an invitation to service expires before the officeholder is ready to relinquish the office.

As in other parts of life, retirement needs to be addressed further upstream. Many boards do not manage their members' expectations well. They allow directors or senior employees to subconsciously conclude that their offices belong to them for life. Anything less is hurtful and potentially disruptive to the director or staff member involved. This can be avoided or at least reduced. Here are some suggestions.

Term limits

I have concluded with some ambivalence that term limits are the best of imperfect options. They are admittedly arbitrary, and sometimes they result in losing the services of someone you would like to retain. They are, nevertheless, in my opinion, better than the alternative. They not only set the stage for rotation, they serve notice that the officeholder has a limited window of time within which to make his/her contribution.

I believe that a member's maximum length of service on a board should be between six and nine years, divided into terms as you will. I have reservations about bringing retired directors back after a year of absence. With rare exceptions, directors have contributed most of what they have to offer within the first six or nine years. The organization will benefit more from new blood.

Criteria for re-upping

Organizations should adopt performance criteria by which incumbent directors qualify to succeed themselves. Re-upping must be earned by performance. Anything less builds mediocrity, or worse, into an organization at the highest level. Determining who qualifies, or who does not qualify, to re-up can so be excruciatingly difficult that it drives some boards to adopt term limits.

The procedure by which incumbent directors are re-upped should demonstrate, in the presence of all, that the invitation is extended with the anticipation of *future* service, not as a reward for *past* service.

Sometimes boards are prevented from retiring mediocre directors because they lack candidates to succeed them. Those responsible to nominate successors (the Board Service Committee) are only too willing to continue an under-performing director just to have a warm body in each chair. This underscores the need to have an active recruitment program that has a list of vetted and qualified directors ready to step in.

Proper treatment of former board members

Look for ways to stay in contact with persons leaving your ranks, other than by adding them to the annual fund-appeal mailing list. Retirees should be invited to special occasions. Some boards share minutes of their meetings with retiring directors for a year after their retirement, softening the loss involved in retirement. Some have an emeritus category for a very select group of retirees. I suggest that such an honor be for a specified period, and not for life.

Habitat for Humanity had the practice of electing former directors and senior employees to an advisory board. When that got unwieldy and seemed to have served its purpose, the Global Leadership Council, composed of selected retirees, replaced it.

Preparing yourself to leave

The responsibility for leaving right does not reside entirely with the organization. Retirees, too, must participate by managing their expectations and preparing something to replace the void which retirement will leave. When tempted to harbor negative thoughts, they must discipline themselves to recall the good times and wish their successors well. Planning for a good retirement is a shared responsibility.

Retirees should be invited to special occasions.

Mennonite Indemnity included in its board service covenant the pledge "… to step aside graciously and with goodwill to my successors and the cause when the time comes."

Leaving right has much to do with leaving at the right time. Leaving right is almost precluded when a director serves one term too long, as some do.

The importance of leaving right was brought home to me when an MCC worker had an emotional breakdown, requiring her to return to the States for treatment. She responded well, but we were taken aback when her therapist recommended that she be permitted to return to her overseas location so that she could "leave right." Leave right? Did the doctor not know, or did he not care, that this involved the expense of an airline ticket halfway around the world? Almost against our better judgment we allowed ourselves to be convinced. It was done, and in retrospect I conclude that we did only what was due her.

Leaving right is important. It is the last thing you want from a service experience.

DISCUSSION QUESTIONS

1. What does your board do to prepare directors or employees for retirement?
2. Do you have criteria for re-upping, or is it assumed and seen as a right?
3. Do you conduct exit interviews with persons who leave your board, inviting their parting thoughts and giving them a brief moment to reflect on their service?
4. What procedures do you have to retain appropriate contact with persons who leave?

Afterword

If you know these things you
are blessed if you do them.

—Jesus to his disciples

Board Self-Evaluation: Board Responsibilities — The Full Scope

KEY

A	B	C	D	E
Strongly agree	Agree	Disagree	Strongly disagree	I don't know

Relationship to Members

1. We have a clear sense of who our members are and what they value and expect.   A B C D E

2. We report to our members in sufficient detail and frequency.   A B C D E

3. We are consciously aware of our fiduciary responsibility to our members.   A B C D E

Board Duties

4. We are clear on our vision and mission, the purpose for which we exist.   A B C D E

5. Working with management, we have an appropriate long-range plan for the future. A B C D E

6. Working with management, we have an annual work plan with identifiable goals. A B C D E

7. We delegate annual work-plan implementation to management/committees with appropriate policies. A B C D E

8. We make sure that financial and personnel resources are reasonably available and assured to complete the annual work plan. A B C D E

9. Working with management, we evaluate program effectiveness annually. A B C D E

Comments: _____

_____

_____

Board Organization and Training

10. We are well served by our officers

    A. Chair: A B C D E

    B. Treasurer: A B C D E

    C. Secretary: A B C D E

11. Our standing committees serve us well. A B C D E

12. A Board Service Committee leads us in evaluating board effectiveness. It anticipates future director and officer needs and brings vetted candidates as needed. A B C D E

13. We have a helpful orientation for new members. [A] [B] [C] [D] [E]

14. We have helpful board-member training activities and events. [A] [B] [C] [D] [E]

Meeting Effectiveness

15. Our board works in a harmonious and trusting atmosphere. [A] [B] [C] [D] [E]

16. Our meetings are orderly and productive. [A] [B] [C] [D] [E]

17. There is full participation in our meetings. [A] [B] [C] [D] [E]

18. Meeting attendance is nearly always complete. [A] [B] [C] [D] [E]

19. The frequency and length of our meetings is about right. [A] [B] [C] [D] [E]

20. Meetings start and adjourn reasonably on time. [A] [B] [C] [D] [E]

21. Our board is skillful in working its way through the agenda and in wrestling and solving tough issues. [A] [B] [C] [D] [E]

22. Our board docket is excellent. It gives us the information we need to do our work. [A] [B] [C] [D] [E]

23. Action items are presented in well-thought-through proposal form. [A] [B] [C] [D] [E]

Relationship with CEO/ and Management

24. There is mutual respect between board and management. [A] [B] [C] [D] [E]

25. The CEO has a job description that states duties and expected outcomes. [A] [B] [C] [D] [E]

26. The board has an annual performance appraisal with its CEO. A B C D E

27. The board supports and cares for its CEO. A B C D E

28. Management and CEO provide requisite, accurate, and objective information as needed. A B C D E

29. The board supplies management with guidance and support as needed without interference. A B C D E

Legal and Financial

30. We have an annual budget, with reporting throughout the year that permits helpful comparisons. A B C D E

31. We have an annual independent financial audit. A B C D E

32. We review the adequacy of our cash and risk management procedures annually. A B C D E

Overall Performance

33. Our overall performance rating is (10=HIGH; 1=LOW) 10 9 8 7 6 5 4 3 2 1

Suggestions for Improvement: _____

_____

_____

_____

Board Self-Evaluation: Board Duties — How Well Are We Accomplishing Them?

Rate how well your board accomplishes its various duties, using a scale from 5 to 1.

KEY

5	4	3	2	1
High				Low

Purpose

How well are we carrying out our legal and
financial obligations?

⑤④③②①

Planning

How effective is our Annual Plan?

⑤④③②①

How current and effective is our Long-Range
Plan?

⑤④③②①

Delegating

How well does the board know which tasks in the
Annual Plan and in the Long-Range Plan are the
its responsibilities? ⑤④③②①

How well does each board committee know what it
is expected to do? ⑤④③②①

How well has the board delegated appropriate tasks
to management by way of the CEO? ⑤④③②①

Board policies

How adequately do they define what is expected of
board committees? ⑤④③②①

How adequately do they define what is expected of
management? ⑤④③②①

Stewardship of Resources

How well does the board steward non-ledger
resources? ⑤④③②①

How well does the board steward the organization's
personnel? ⑤④③②①

How well does the board steward the organization's
reputation? ⑤④③②①

How well does the board steward ledger resources? ⑤④③②①

How well does the board steward its budget
process? ⑤④③②①

How well does the board steward its audit process? ⑤④③②①

How well does the board steward physical plant
and equipment? ⑤④③②①

Monitoring and Evaluating

How well does the board know what is going on in the organization?   5 4 3 2 1

Does the board know what the outcomes of the organization's work are?   5 4 3 2 1

Reporting back to the membership

How well do board and staff keep the organization's membership informed?   5 4 3 2 1

How well do you celebrate accomplishments/ anniversaries?   5 4 3 2 1

Overall performance   5 4 3 2 1

_____   _____

DIRECTOR'S NAME   DATE

EXHIBIT C

Board Self-Evaluation: Board Meetings — Our Work Together

Consider how effective you are as an individual director. Consider how well your full board works at its task collectively. Use the scale below to assess performance, and write brief answers when more extended comments are requested.

KEY

5	4	3	2	1
High				Low

1. How do you rate your performance as a director?   5 4 3 2 1

   State 3 specific things you plan to do in the next year to improve your performance as a director.

   1 _____

   2 _____

   3 _____

EXHIBIT C — BOARD SELF-EVALUATION: BOARD MEETINGS

2. How do you rate the performance of the committee on which you serve?   5 4 3 2 1

   Name of committee: _____

   Suggestions for improvement: _____

   _____

3. Please state your opinion about each of the following in regards to board meetings:

   Frequency _____

   Length _____

   Venue/Facilities _____

   Agenda and distribution of meeting time _____

   _____

4. Performance of the board chair:

   Conducting meetings   5 4 3 2 1

   Suggestions for improvement: _____

   _____

   Between-meetings performance   5 4 3 2 1

   Suggestions for improvement: _____

   _____

5. Adequacy and accuracy of the minute record   5 4 3 2 1

   Suggestions for improvement: _____

   _____

6. Accuracy and adequacy of financial reporting 5 4 3 2 1

   Suggestions for improvement: _____

   _____

7. Staff performance related to assisting board function:

   Adequacy of reporting 5 4 3 2 1

   Skill in identifying issues for board action 5 4 3 2 1

   Skill in bringing actionable proposals for board 5 4 3 2 1
   action

   Overall quality of relationship between board 5 4 3 2 1
   and staff

8. How well is the board doing its governance job? 5 4 3 2 1

   Suggestions for improvement: _____

   _____

_____   _____

DIRECTOR'S NAME   DATE

_____

Director Self-Evaluation

1. Your name _____

2. Year elected _____

3. Percentage of board meetings attended _____

4. Level of satisfaction: On a continuum, where   5 4 3 2 1
   5 is *deeply satisfying* and 1 is a *waste of time,*
   how would you rate the level of satisfaction
   you get by serving on this board?

   Observations/suggestions: _____

5. Committee Service: Name the committee(s) on which you
   serve. Rank the committees' effectiveness.

   A _____   5 4 3 2 1

   Observations/suggestions: _____

   _____

   B _____   5 4 3 2 1

   Observations/suggestions: _____

   _____

6. Rank your own performance as a board member ⑤ ④ ③ ② ①

   List the particular contributions and strengths you believe you bring to the board: _____

   _____

   State your personal goals and resolutions for improving and increasing your effectiveness on this board: _____

   _____

7. Are you willing to serve another term if asked? Why? _____

   _____

8. Name the committee assignment(s) you prefer: _____

   _____

   _____
   DATE

Suggestions for Committees

"**C**ommittee meetings," a cynic has said, "is where you keep minutes and lose hours." Sometimes that happens because assignments and expectations are not well defined. Here, briefly, are guidelines for maximizing a committee's time and energy.

Committee appointment is by the board upon the recommendation of the Chair. Members may offer nominations or volunteer themselves, but appointment is by the board.

Term of service. Appointment is for the duration of the assignment, or from year-to-year, renewable by board action.

Job description. Committees are given a general description of what is expected. From this they are expected to draw up a more comprehensive job description, stating what they wish to accomplish, why they should exist. They should submit this to the board for approval.

Work plan. Each year, committees should be asked to present to the board through the Chair a work plan that identifies the issues they propose to address that year. The board may also make assignments to committees.

Authority. Board committees are responsible to the board. They have only the authority that is expressly given to them by the board.

Committees do not make decisions for the board; they help the board with its decision-making.

Committee meetings. Committees are free to schedule meetings as they deem necessary.

Meeting notice and preparation. The board Chair and CEO should be included in the meeting call and distribution of agenda.

Minutes. A complete and accurate summary of each meeting should be available within three days of a meeting. The minutes should be shared with all who participated, plus the board Chair and CEO and all others affected by the committee's work. Appropriate exception should be made for confidential matters.

Reporting to the board. A report should state at the outset which of the following three kinds of reports it is:

1. A progress report. FYI only. No action expected.
2. A query or request for counsel. Opportunity for input but no firm decision expected.
3. A recommendation for board approval. Aim to write the recommendation in such a manner that it can, subject to board approval, be read right into the minutes.

Recommendations should have been cleared ahead of time with others who will be affected by them.

A proposed recommendation should not exceed one page in length, with attachments as necessary. It should be available for distribution with the agenda and the board docket.

A Reminder: Committees must guard against taking on a life of their own. They must be careful not to usurp the authority of the CEO nor end up focusing below the line. Continuous effort must be made to coordinate their work with other board committees.

Writing Effective Proposals for Board Action

A proposal gathers together the main elements of an issue and recommends a course of action. Great boards require that all major subjects be presented in proposal form. This applies to board committees as well as to management.

The following is an example of a proposal prepared for board action. Note the elements it includes—background information, a work plan, a recommended board action, and a comment about the proposal's effect on budget.

To: Board of Directors A RECOMMENDATION FOR ACTION
From: Xxxx Xxxx, CEO
RE: Tree planting
Date: Xxx, Xxx

I did a windshield survey of the more than 100 houses Habitat has built in this city. I was surprised to discover that less than 10% have any trees on the premises. I remind myself that

- Habitat is about more than houses. We are concerned with the habitat within which people live, and trees are part of that habitat.
- Trees cause property values to increase.
- Trees add to quality of life; they add beauty and serve as nature's air conditioner.
- Trees are good for the environment.

On my way home, I stopped at the Green Tree Nursery (GTN) where I spoke to Mr. Walker, the President. He was immediately interested in what I reported, and together we came up with what we think is a workable plan.

- GTN will make available and plant (but not guarantee) 50 ten-foot maple trees at the subsidized price of $25 each.
- The Habitat homeowner will A.) dig a hole three feet deep and three feet in diameter, B.) commit to watering the tree as necessary throughout the summer, and C.) pay $25 per tree at the time of planting.
- Habitat will promote the project to homeowners and will coordinate planting.

RECOMMENDATION: That staff be authorized to move ahead with a tree-planting project for Habitat homeowners along the lines presented in the proposal as attached in Exhibit 3 in the Board docket. This will, in the first stage, be limited to 50 homeowners on a first-come first-served basis, but a second phase may be considered if there is sufficient interest. It is further recommended that at least one tree be included in all future family house projects.

(The plan is budget neutral. The construction staff will manage the project. Tree planting will take place next spring.)

The proposal informs the directors at the outset that action is expected. It goes on to identify the issue being addressed. It then states what action is being proposed and concludes with a one-paragraph recommendation. In short, it tells the board everything it needs to know to act on this recommendation.

If the board is in agreement, it simply adopts the recommendation, which is then read right into the minutes of the meeting, facilitating minute-taking. Proposals permit a board to make a decision in minutes that would otherwise take hours.

The board always has the prerogative to change what is being recommended. In this illustration, it may increase or decrease the number of trees in the project. It may increase or decrease the amount the homeowner is asked to pay, or it may scrap the idea altogether for whatever reason. The proposal simply introduces the idea and suggests a course of action. It helps the board to focus its attention more quickly, leading to better decisions.

Staff and committees must learn to prepare their material in proposal form. Great boards learn how to process written proposals.

CEO Annual Review Outline

Note that I call this an annual review, not a performance appraisal. I mean to suggest a two-way *conversation*, in contrast to a performance appraisal in which the CEO is more of an object than a conversation partner.

It is assumed that the review is initiated by the board Chair, to whom the CEO is responsible, with another director present. This can be the Board Service Committee Chair or another director designated by the board. That director is present simply to provide the objectivity of a witness.

The Chair's Pre-Interview Check list

1. Review the job description. What is the CEO asked to do?
2. Review the written summary of previous reviews.
3. Schedule the annual review with the CEO in a comfortable setting, free of interruptions. Inform him/her how you plan to proceed, maybe even giving in advance a copy of the outline you plan to use. There should be no surprises. I suggest 90 minutes, allowing for some spontaneous discussion that might ensue.

4. Invite comment from the board in an executive session. Note both commendations/concerns.
5. Invite comment from senior staff who report to the CEO. Get a general sense of the rapport the CEO has with staff. Listen, but not do respond. Be careful not to undercut the CEO. Do not show agreement or disapproval with information they volunteer. The key word is *listen*.

The Interview

Make some effort to put the CEO at ease.
1. Invite the CEO to reflect on the past year, especially regarding:
    - Highlights
    - Disappointments
    - Staff support
    - Relationship with the board
    - Level of satisfaction in his/her position
2. Next, as board Chair, reflect on the past year, stating both accomplishments and disappointments from the board's perspective. You *must* openly discuss areas in which improvement is needed, but do it constructively, thoughtfully, sensitively. Invite response. Be interactive. A secure CEO will receive criticism as an opportunity to improve performance and relationships, if approached appropriately.
3. Show personal interest in the CEO but respect his/her privacy. You might make a general inquiry about the following and allow the CEO to decide at what depth to respond.
    - How the kids are doing
    - Hobbies (golf score?)
    - Health—maybe inquire when s/he had her/his last physical examination
    - Plans for a leave or studies to upgrade skills
    - Future plans

4. Take some time to anticipate, to dream together, about what the next year will require by way of executive leadership. Identify priorities and challenges which you both anticipate.

Post-Interview

Prepare a written summary of the interview, covering both affirmations and areas where adjustments are needed. These summaries are hard to write, but necessary. Be specific about areas where performance needs to be improved. Conclude the summary by giving the CEO 10 days either to accept your summary or to make his/her own statement, after which the written exchange will be shared with the board in executive session.

Make every effort to make this a positive experience, even if (especially if!) there are sensitive points. This post-interview summary can enhance the relationship of the board and its CEO.

Desired Outcome

You want to conclude by appealing to team spirit: We know who we are and what we are about. We know our respective roles and we intend to discharge them. We are in this together. Ours is, in the truest sense, a partnership characterized by mutual respect and trust.

A Qualifier

When the relationship between the board and the CEO is stable, a 360-degree review such as I have described above may not be necessary annually. It can, in fact, be distracting. My old boss used to say that you can pull the potato up only so many times before you interfere with its growth. In such a healthy relationship, I urge as a minimum an annual "conversation" between the board Chair (preferably with another member present). This provides an opportunity to check signals and plot strategy. The 360-degree review should then be done every second or third year.

Annual Salary Review

Some boards combine the salary review with the annual review, while others separate them. I do not have a strong preference. What is important is that the salary is reviewed annually in a thoughtful manner. Nonprofits that are not in a position to pay the prevailing wage should not compound the issue by leaving their CEO feeling taken for granted or left dangling. Genuine care and thoughtfulness transcend salary, although the salary must afford a reasonable standard of living if the relationship is intended to continue.

If all of this seems like heavy work, it is. But few things are more important than a good board/CEO working relationship.

CEO Search Checklist

1.   The board is in charge of the process of finding a successor. It is not the task of the outgoing CEO. You may invite his/her opinion on appropriate details, and you should keep him/her generally informed. But the point is, choosing a CEO is board responsibility, unless and until it is delegated.

2.   Determine when the position is open. This is the first point in arriving at a timetable. Ideally, boards like to have (but seldom get) most of nine to 12 months to complete the process. In some cases, it is better to have an interim CEO rather than to rush things.

3.   Appoint a Search Committee and include a timetable. I suggest that three members make up the committee, and not more than five. Ideally, they should be directors with Human Resource (HR) experience; sometimes a carefully selected employee may be added to the committee. If the board is very inexperienced with searches, it may be wise to invite a professional HR person, who is not a director but a friend of the cause, to serve as a consultant.

4.   Draw up a job description that states the duties assigned to the position and the expected outcomes.

5.   Draw up the terms and qualifications, addressing:
     • educational requirements and/or degrees

- values
- experience and demonstrated competencies
- salary and benefits

6. Announce and/or advertise the position and invite candidates. Throw the net wide.

7. The Search Committee evaluates the list of candidates against the stated terms and qualifications. It eliminates candidates in which it is not interested and interviews the rest. From this, the Committee draws up a short list of candidates—not more than three—and vets them thoroughly, including the following for each:
    - Police check
    - Credit rating
    - Church or pastor reference
    - Previous employment references (subject to the candidate's prior approval)
    - Personal interview, including the board Chair. Be prepared to hand the candidates a packet that includes such vital material as Vision and Mission statements, program and budget summaries, board-member roster, job description, and so on.

8. The Search Committee narrows the search to one candidate. At this stage, some boards request the candidate to take a psychological and/or occupational test to help establish his/her suitability for the job and as a safety measure of sorts.

9. The Search Committee presents the candidate it is recommending to the board, along with background information, on a confidential basis. The Search Committee also arranges for the candidate to interact with the board and senior staff and invites comments. Senior staff are not invited to vote on the candidate.

10. If the board approves, and if staff comments are favorable, the Search Committee consummates the understanding with the candidate and presents him/her to the board for appointment. The candidate is announced and installed.

If the Search Committee's candidate is not confirmed, the committee returns to its short list and repeats the process. An overlap of six to eight weeks with the outgoing CEO is normally adequate.

11. The unsuccessful candidates are thanked.
12. The Search Committee is thanked and dismissed.

There are circumstances when it is appropriate to engage a professional search firm.

EXHIBIT I

Suggestions for Interviewing a Candidate for the CEO Position

1. Organize yourselves before the interview. Some committees appoint one member to lead the interview, while others distribute the interview questions among the members of the Search Committee so each can participate in the questioning. Schedule some space between appointments so you have time to check signals and so candidates don't run into each other.

2. Invite each candidate to tell about him/herself. Listen for information, but, even more, look for personality traits. Observe personal warmth or lack of it. Observe evidence of self-confidence or lack of it. Do you detect arrogance? Allow candidates to present themselves as they are.

3. Ask questions that pertain to the competencies needed to fulfill the job description and which are experience-based, not hypothetical. If this includes fund-raising, ask the candidate to tell about when s/he raised funds for a particular cause. If planning is a priority, ask her/him to tell about an activity s/he has planned.

This is not an entry-level position. A CEO must be able to hit the ground running.

4.   Ask open-ended questions. For example, Tell us about a time when you dealt with low morale among employees. Tell us about an experience in which you had a difference of opinion with a board or a boss. What books you have read in the past months?

5.   Laws prohibit you from asking questions that are not related to the job for which candidates are interviewing. You are not permitted to ask about age, health, marital status, or number of children. You may not ask directly about church or political-party affiliation unless it is related to the job. Some of this information may arise from the interview spontaneously, but you must not intrude on the privacy of the interviewee.

6.   Look for a match. Is this person comfortable with us? Will we be comfortable with her/him? Are our values similar or compatible? Look not only at what the candidates have done, or at how they present themselves in the interviews, but look also for signs of growth potential. Allow for intangibles (those traits you sense but cannot adequately explain or express).

7.   Some Search Committees use a spreadsheet which lists the traits required to fulfill the job description and assigns a value to each, totaling 100. If you have five traits, you may assign each one 20 points, or, because one is so important you may assign it 40 points and spread the remaining 60 points over the other four traits. One trait may be "Intangibles." In this way, each member of the Search Committee assigns points as they interview multiple candidates. In the end, all the scores are totaled, revealing which candidates have risen to the top of the list.

8.   Don't fail to allow the candidates to ask questions of you. Much can be learned by what they ask and how they ask.

Governance Guidelines: A Model for a Start-Up Organization

(To be filed in the Policy Manual and given to new board members at their orientation.)

I use Bridge of Hope National (BOHN) and its board of directors (BOD) as my model for a start-up.

1. **Introduction:** The BOHN BOD is guided first by its bylaws. Basically, it will operate according to *Robert's Rules of Order*, as adapted for use in a smaller assembly.

2. **Board Responsibility:** The BOD can and will delegate functions, but the responsibility for what does or does not happen rests with the BOD.

3. **Meeting Attendance:** Directors are expected to attend all board and committee meetings. When unable to attend a meeting, directors are expected to ask to be excused. Two consecutive unexcused absences constitute disqualification from the board.

4. **Meeting Participation:** Directors are expected to read materials distributed in advance. They are expected to address and interact with each other in a respectful manner. This also applies to disagreements. Routine business will be transacted by consent.

5. **Agenda:** Board meeting agendas are prepared jointly by the board Chair and CEO and distributed in advance.

6. **Meeting Frequency:** The BOD will meet quarterly. Additional meetings may be called by the Chair and the Secretary as the need arises. It is expected that the Chair and the CEO will meet at least once between meetings of the board.

7. **Reporting:** The CEO will keep the BOD well informed through written reports, and otherwise as necessary. Written reports will be shared with the BOD at least one week before the regular meeting.

8. **Payment:** Directors serve gratis. Expenses related to meeting attendance or assignments are reimbursable.

9. **Confidentiality:** The BOD is committed to do its business in an atmosphere of trust and openness. Where confidentiality is required, directors pledge to uphold it conscientiously.

10. **Conflict of Interest:** Directors are expected to act in the best interests of BOHN. Directors are expected to recuse themselves from participating with items in which they have conflicting interests.

11. **Use of Committees:** BOHN operates from a principle of board wholeness. Committees may be used for special assignments and/or to prepare issues for action by the BOD. Committees have only the authority given to them by the board. Committees shall prepare and promptly distribute a record of all meetings to the entire board.

12. **Evaluation:** The BOD will do a performance self-evaluation annually and an annual performance appraisal of the CEO. Program evaluation will be part of the annual planning process.

13. **Policies:** The BOD is committed to doing its work, as much as practical, from a policy perspective. To that end, it will create a Board Policy Manual where all board policies will be filed and

readily available for consultation. The responsibility for updating this Manual annually is assigned to the Secretary of the BOD, working with the CEO.

14. **Recommendations/Written Proposals:** Major issues needing board action shall be presented in recommendation/proposal form. This applies both to management and to board committees.

Thoughts for Reflection

The greatest danger facing all of us is
  not that we should make an absolute failure of life,
  nor that we should fall into outright licentiousness,
  nor that we should be terribly unhappy,
  nor that we will find that life has no meaning
    —not any of these.

The danger is that we may
  fail to perceive life's greatest meaning,
  fall short of its highest good,
  miss its deepest and most abiding happiness,
  be unable to render the most needed service,
  be unconscious of life ablaze with the light of God's
  presence, and be content to have it so
    —that is the danger.

That some day we may wake up and find that always we have
been busy with the husks and trapping of life—and have missed
life itself. For life without God, to one who has known the rich-
ness and joy of life with him, is unthinkable, impossible.

That is what one prays to be spared—satisfaction with a life that falls short of the best, that has in it no tingle and thrill which comes from friendship with the Father.

—Phillips Brooks,
AMERICAN HYMN WRITER

He who has received much that is good and beautiful in life must give appropriately in return. He who is spared personal suffering must realize that he is called upon to help alleviate the suffering of others. We must all share in carrying the burden of pain laid upon the world.

—Dr. Albert Schweitzer
MISSIONARY DOCTOR AND MUSICIAN

About the Author

Edgar Stoesz has spent most of his adult life in nonprofit organizations, both as director and employee. A native Minnesotan, he held six different administrative posts with the Mennonite Central Committee, including seven years as Associate Executive Secretary. For 38 years he served as President/CEO of Mennonite Indemnity, a for profit reinsurance company serving mutual insurance companies.

He has been active on the board of Habitat for Humanity, International, serving as Chair from 1991 to 1995. Additionally he has chaired the boards of Heifer Project, International; the American Leprosy Mission; and Hospital Albert Schweitzer. He has served on numerous other local and national boards, including Mennonite Economic Development Associates.

Since co-authoring the widely acclaimed book, *Doing Good Better* in 1995, Stoesz has addressed or conducted workshops for more than 150 boards. He has also written *Common Sense for Board Members* and edited the collection, *Meditations for Meetings: Thoughtful Meditations for Board Meetings and for Leaders*, all published by Good Books.

METHOD OF PAYMENT

❑ Check or Money Order
*(payable to **Good Books** in U.S. funds)*

❑ Please charge my:

    ❑ MasterCard ❑ Visa
    ❑ Discover   ❑ American Express

\# _____

exp. date _____

Signature _____

Name _____

Address _____

City _____

State _____

Zip _____

Phone _____

Email _____

SHIP TO: (if different)

Name _____

Address _____

City _____

State _____

Zip _____

Mail order to: **Good Books**
P.O. Box 419 • Intercourse, PA 17534-0419
Call toll-free: 800/762-7171
Fax toll-free: 888/768-3433
Prices subject to change.

Doing Good Even Better
ORDER FORM

If you would like to order copies of **Doing Good Even Better** for boards you know or are part of, use this form. (Discounts apply only for more than one copy.)

Photocopy this page as often as you like.

The following discounts apply:

1 copy	$9.95
2-5 copies	$8.96 each (a 10% discount)
6-10 copies	$8.46 each (a 15% discount)
11-20 copies	$7.96 each (a 20% discount)

To order larger quantities, please call 800/762-7171 for discounts.

Prices subject to change.

Quantity   Price   Total

_____ copies of **Doing Good Even Better** @ _____ _____

PA residents add 6% sales tax _____

Shipping & Handling
(add 10%; $3.00 minimum) _____

TOTAL _____

(Please fill in the payment and shipping information on the other side.)